# LIVING WITHOUT LIMITS

## *a memoir by Andi Jones*

Copyright © 2015 by Andi Jones

All rights reserved. In accordance with the U.S. Copyright Act of 1976, the scanning, uploading and electronic sharing of any part of this book without the permission of the publisher is unlawful piracy and theft of the author's intellectual property. If you would like to use material from the book, other than for review purposes, prior written permission must be obtained by contacting the author at mountainliving2018@gmail.com. Thank you for your support of the author's rights.

This author has a blog at [ironmanandi.blogspot.com](ironmanandi.blogspot.com)

## A NOTE FROM THE AUTHOR

If I could have seen into my future, fifteen years ago, I would have insisted something was mistaken. I had no aspirations to leave my comfort zone and challenge my perception of what I could or could not do. Then I realized I may be stealing my own potential and found the courage to face my fear of taking chemistry, which ultimately led me through challenges while pursuing unimaginable dreams.

Accomplishing any goal requires a first step towards it and sometimes that step is the hardest. As we move forward, it is important to use our energy to work through obstacles, rather than make excuses. Obstacles are opportunities that either strengthen our drive to achieve a goal, or empower a perceived limit, making us miss what may be around the corner. I know I missed seeing what was around many corners, until I recognized I was my biggest obstacle and found the courage to face myself and make a change. We need to dream beyond perceived limits and find the courage to pursue those dreams.

# TABLE OF CONTENTS

STEALING MY LIFE

FACING MY DEMON

NURSING DREAM

COURAGE OF OTHERS

MY ENDURANCE EVENT

RUNNING FOR FUN

IRONMAN THOUGHTS

UNEXPECTED CHALLENGE

IRONMAN ARIZONA

REACHING FOR A STAR

LOTTERY HANGOVER

VISUALIZATION FINDS A HOME

IRONMAN WORLD CHAMPIONSHIP

# STEALING MY LIFE

*"Let no one steal away your life while you are still breathing. Most of all, pray that the thief will not be you."– Taylor Hartman, Ph.D*

Nobody enjoys failing, but some of us are better at recovering from it than others. I was well into my thirties before I noticed the fortress my sub consciousness had built to protect me from failure. I learned in my youth that failure hurts and, somehow, unbeknownst to my conscious self, I learned how to avoid it at all costs. My last attempt at something that could invoke failure was almost 30 years ago, when I tried to walk on to my local university's women's basketball team and didn't make it. After that, I made my way into the safe, inner place my sub consciousness had prepared and started learning how to be happy avoiding any potential failure.

I found a safe, administrative position to help put me through school. I planned to become a Speech Therapist, but when I learned it required a Master's degree, I convinced myself I would be happy simply getting a Bachelor's degree and keep working in my administrative job. Pursuing a graduate degree may broach the "failure zone" and I didn't want to be there.

I was a dedicated, responsible, committed employee and learned those qualities were a recipe for success. I moved quickly up a lucrative ladder which made it easy to continue working there. I enjoyed the people with whom I worked and felt appreciated by my supervisors. I had it made; I worked nine to five in a place where failure was nowhere within my sight.

I had settled in, enjoying my life, until one evening when I read something about strengths and weaknesses within different personalities. A thought caught my attention about being careful that our life not be stolen away from ourselves, and particularly that the thief not be ourself. This struck me hard... I felt my breath leave my body. Was I stealing away my potential by being so fearful of failing? I shook my head and forced that thought out of my mind. It was too much to think about. I was living a safe life because that is what was best for me, right?

The next morning I awoke with that thought still in my head. I regressed to my earlier school years and remembered I had tried living my life to a greater potential, but the middle school coach had put me in my place for three consecutive years and I learned I wasn't good enough. I paused and recognized I had been empowering others' perceptions of my abilities and owning them as my own. Having recognized this, what would I do?

A dear friend of mine, thirty-five years my senior, gave me some poignant advice when I worked with her years ago. She had aspirations to be an artist, but had been such a good loan officer that, before she knew it, she was in her 50's and felt trapped within her job. I remembered this advice and realized I was headed down a career path that would both keep me in a safe place, as well as keep me from realizing my potential.

> ***Living without Limits:*** *When thoughts come together and point towards change, attend to what triggered them and courageously consider taking action.*

# FACING MY DEMON

*Mental energy is powerful. We should direct its strength
towards our positive aspirations rather than empowering
unsubstantiated fears.*

The innermost part of me had always admired nurses; they seemed to know just what to do. I had worked with an ambulance company and dropped off patients in the hands of capable nurses and learned to envy their knowledge and confidence. Nursing was what I was born to be, but my fear of taking chemistry classes stood between me and pursuing my dream.

My mind had turned Chemistry into a monster, an unconquerable demon to whom I was destined to fail! I wish there was some explanation or personal experience why I felt like this, but as hard as I try I can't come up with one. I simply didn't want to take Chemistry and, as the years passed, it seemed to get worse and worse in my head. It was my understandable, internal excuse of why I had pursued a Speech Therapy degree instead of Nursing.

I had a new perspective and could not deny it was me holding myself back from pursuing a nursing degree; all because of my fear of Chemistry. I could stay in my current job and make a fine living at it, but the cost would be giving up my dream. This sounded like my loan officer friend and I knew what her advice would be… find the courage to follow my dream.

I was in my late 30's and being presented with the idea of stepping out of my safe, non-failure zone, where I had safely existed for almost twenty years. The cost of which would be to give up my secure, comfortable job, where I was the expert, and go back to school, as a full time student, where I would be the one asking the questions.

I processed the thought of jumping from my administrative position into the realm of student life, and realized I would regret not challenging my perceived limits. The best way to get out of my safe, protected living area was to close my eyes and jump with both feet, which is exactly what I did. I registered for Chemistry and prepared for a big change.

When I found myself back in school, I panicked for a short while and then remembered what my end goal was. I focused on maintaining a positive mindset and taking each class one at a time. Nursing school was still months away, but I had found the courage to drastically change my direction towards a goal with the potential to change my life and it felt so right.

> ***Living without Limits:*** *Our comfort zones are so appealing and appear to be the best place for us, until something helps us discover they are wolves in sheep's clothing and our potential is passing us by.*

# NURSING DREAM

*Rejection in my early life cultivated complacency and I learned to ignore my dreams. I knew they were there, but ignoring them kept me from feeling the hurt of more rejection.*

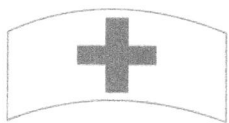

I was accepted into nursing school and became a Registered Nurse. It didn't take me long to recognize that nursing is a privilege; which other profession both helps bring newborns into this world, and compassionately comforts the elderly as they realize their time to depart is nearing. During nursing school I experienced so much:

- I sat on the bed with my 4-year-old patient and played card games.
- I cleaned up messes and smelled smells that I never knew existed.
- I tiptoed around sterile fields hoping I would not contaminate anything.
- I bathed a newborn baby and tenderly handed him to his tentative, new father.
- I found myself comforting a mother and father who were preparing to give birth to their stillborn child.
- I listened to and consoled the wife of my 94-year-old patient as she wondered how she was going to live alone after being with her sweetheart for 65 years.
- My fingers were finally squeezed by the professional skier after being in a coma for weeks.
- My calm breathing carefully coached the anxious breaths of the teenager whose burns were being painfully cleaned.
- I played "catcher" as a very sick newborn was passed through the window into the Newborn Intensive Care Unit.
- I sat with the parents of their brain-dead son as they decided he would indeed want to be a donor if he could prolong another's life.

- I was with the recipient of a heart transplant as he realized he would indeed spend many more active years with his children.

Some of these experiences challenged my potential, but they prepared me for what it is really like to be a nurse. I believe it takes an extraordinary person to be a consistently exceptional nurse. It can be exhausting, but every shift I make decisions that directly affect my patients' lives. I am honored to recommit each shift to have the courage to implement my personal values and truly be my patients' advocate. I will do all I can to remember why I initially pursued this challenging career that provides me an understanding and appreciation of life that few other professions offer.

I look back on what I would have missed if I had chosen to stay at my administrative job and I shake my head. I almost let a chemistry class keep me from making a difference in people's lives. Thank goodness I recognized I was stealing away my life and found the courage to do something about it.

> ***Living without Limits:*** *Jumping out of my comfort zone and making it through nursing school showed me my worth, allowing me to move past previous rejection and embrace newfound potential.*

# COURAGE OF OTHERS

*Sometimes simple decisions lead to courageous actions which inspire others.*

After experiencing the rewards of stepping out of my comfort zone, I developed a newfound confidence. Nursing school taught me what it feels like to try something I wasn't sure I would be able to accomplish. Shortly after I graduated, my good friend Natalie shared she was embarking upon her own challenging goal; she had registered to participate in an ironman distance triathlon.

When she shared her desire to participate in an Ironman, I had little idea what it meant. I learned it consisted of a 2.4 mile swim, followed by a 112 mile bike ride and then a 26.2 mile run, and you had to finish all that before midnight. Some friends and I traveled to support her and, at that time, the importance of witnessing this event in person was unbeknownst to me. Natalie's courageous decision to participate in an Ironman would ultimately affect my soul.

None of us knew what to expect on race day. We were all Ironman virgins, blank pages, waiting to see what the day would bring. We had no idea how we would be changed after nineteen hours of waiting, wondering, cheering, worrying, calculating and, most of all, simply feeling.

The great feeling of accomplishing a difficult goal was still present in my heart and I hoped to see Natalie feel it too. We got an early start and perched ourselves on a concrete wall, high enough to see above anyone who might stand below us. We shared words of encouragement with Natalie as she left to begin her adventure.

I have never experienced anything like watching that swim. I was surprised by the emotion involved in the entire event, but the mass start of the swim was particularly stunning. I watched hundreds of athletes stream into the lake to start a swim that could last over two hours. It was a unique experience to watch humans make their way into a huge, cold lake and be transformed into what looked like thousands of fish fins.

I was speechless; no words could describe the feeling as the last athletes made their way into the water. It quickly became apparent that this day would be like none other. I literally sat in silence, in awe of what I was witnessing. I felt tears stream down my cheeks and looked to see I was not the only one experiencing these emotions. We sat there in an unexpected, dazed state. As we gathered our emotions and explored this unrealistic reality, athletes started coming out of the water to begin their second lap. You see, all these athletes had to swim not just one, but two laps of what seemed like an impossible distance.

None of us had any idea what it must feel like to swim in open water, with that many people, for that amount of time. All the unknown information was helping my natural worrier friends increase any tension we non-worriers were already experiencing. It was a new experience for each of us, in so many unexpected ways.

We finally saw Natalie come out of the water. She stood up, put her arm in the air and looked at us with an exhausted, "oh my" look on her face which was quickly replaced with a smile. She did it! She finished the swim and we were all relieved.

These athletes who had just finished swimming 2.4 miles were now headed out for a 112 mile bike ride. I couldn't get my head around that thought. We scattered to keep Natalie in sight and soon saw her running with her bike in one hand and a peanut butter and jelly sandwich in the other one. She saw us, waved and headed out on her bike.

It is still difficult to find words to describe that swim. It was mesmerizing to watch so many athletes stream into the water and swim side by side for so long. I could only imagine the type of preparation it required to do something so courageous. I started to recognize that Ironman athletes were something special and felt humbled to be in their presence.

We found a curb along the course where we could cheer for the athletes and take in the unique feelings surrounding the Ironman. I was awestruck by the variety of sizes, shapes, and ages of athletes who passed by us. There weren't only lean, trim athletic humans trying to accomplish this event, there were short, tall, big, small, wide, thin, old and young making their way through the course. I found myself admiring these amazing people who were obviously putting themselves to the test. Don't get me wrong, there were very lean, athletic competitors, tearing through the course, but I expected to see that type of athlete. It was the less typical looking athletes who made an impression upon me; an impression that would last well beyond that particular day. How were those athletes able to do what they were doing?

It was time to start watching for Natalie. We made a noble attempt to estimate how long it would take her, but that time came and went. We shouldn't have been surprised because of the heat and distance they were riding, but we wondered if everything was alright. We had seen ambulances transporting athletes to the medical area, which hinted that Ironman racing was not a benign sport. We continued waiting, hoping desperately to see her.

There are time cutoffs for each sport in Ironman races. Athletes have to be done with the bike and start running by 5:30 p.m. or their quest to finish an Ironman would end prematurely. The cutoff time kept getting closer and closer with no sign of Natalie. There were fewer cyclists on the course, which added to our stress. Waiting was hard because we didn't know where she was on the course. All we could do was hope nothing had gone wrong.

Our waiting finally paid off, as she rounded the corner and coasted to the finish. Her head was down and there was no smile on her face; she looked exhausted. It was a welcomed relief to see her, but I instantly wanted to help because of how uncomfortable she appeared. My logical mind realized she had about 30 minutes to start her run, or her day would end. I wondered if she would make it.

I experienced a strong sense of helplessness. There are obviously more intense situations of helplessness, but I felt like my hands were tied. I wanted to help, but instead had to trust that the volunteers knew what she needed and would get her back on the course before the cutoff so she could continue pursuing her goal.

My helplessness led me to do the only thing I knew I could do, I hurried and got as close as I could to the changing tent. A couple of us watched for her to come out, but there was no sign of her and it was getting dangerously close to the cutoff time. We embarrassingly yelled her name, hoping she would hear us and sense the urgency. We continued calling out as desperate friends, needing to know she was alright and that she knew she should hurry. This makes me laugh now, as I better understand she was very aware of the time and had volunteers reminding her of the urgency. We were doing all we could to feel like we were helping.

Finally an athlete slowly walked out of the tent and it was Natalie. Surely she had heard us yelling her name and would look for her faithful friends…nope. She was headed away from us, so we hollered her name and she turned towards us. She looked tired and dazed. She walked to us and said she was happy to be off her bike. Little did she know that we felt the same! We talked with her until she exited the area and officially started her marathon. Whew!

Ironman spectating was already exhausting and we still had a marathon to go. We watched the sun lower out of the sky and realized the athletes had been on the move since just after sunrise, striving for one common goal. I couldn't get my mind around that concept. It was truly inspiring to see all sizes and shapes of athletes striving to accomplish the same thing.

Waiting during the marathon was another new challenge for me. I felt I needed to do something, so I got help calculating how fast Natalie needed to continue moving to be able to finish before midnight. When we saw her again, we shared our calculations and she asked if she could walk; our answer was an emphatic no. She didn't like our immediate answer, but she was cutting it close. We reminded her to keep moving forward, as quickly as she could, and she left to continue her quest to finish an Ironman.

The run course took the athletes well away from the finish area, so we had no idea how she was doing, which was frustrating. I passed time by walking up and down the approach to the finish and happily cheered for those running down that last section. There was an inspirational feeling as each athlete found the energy to actually run towards the finish, even after what they had been doing all day. Unbelievable!

It kept getting later and later which meant the midnight deadline was getting closer and closer. I tried not to look at my watch too often because time was moving so slowly. We had been waiting and watching all day and now it was down to minutes. Some of us made our way further up the course to hopefully find our friend. I stopped at a corner to cheer for athletes as they passed. Eventually my focus on what time it was disappeared and was replaced by a unique energy from witnessing what was happening along those dark streets. There was a permeating energy as Ironman athletes made their way past me, within one mile from what they had been striving for all day, literally all day! I found my eyes filling with tears. I had never experienced anything like this; it was most powerful while sitting on the curb, alone, in the dark, giving words of encouragement to athletes as they passed me. Some were alone, others were alongside a fellow athlete they met along the run and found encouragement from each other as they struggled towards their common goal, the Ironman finish line. What must this last mile feel like after fighting so hard for it all day long?

I saw our group quickly heading towards me, saying they found Natalie and were hurrying to make it to the finish. I stayed where I was, waiting to see my amazing, courageous friend, so I could quietly tell her how proud I was of her and that she was going to make it. She came around the corner and I stayed on the sidewalk, away from the actual course, talking with her as I quickened my pace. I hoped it would help her speed up because it was ever so close to midnight. I wanted so badly to go right by her side, but I respected the solidarity of the Ironman which challenges athletes to work through every minute on their own. I said what I wanted to and rushed forward, telling her I'd see her at the finish.

I ran to the bleachers along the finish chute and shortly after I stopped, I saw Natalie cross the finish line and heard her name announced as an official Ironman finisher.

We had been at the Ironman the entire day and had our own experience being Ironman spectators. It was something else to wait and wonder for almost seventeen hours, not knowing how Natalie was doing, wanting so badly to help, but knowing she had to do it on her own. She was persistent and met the challenges before her, as did hundreds of fellow athletes putting their limits to the test. I had witnessed an incredible show of courage, determination, dedication and belief.

> ***Living without Limits:*** *Watching an Ironman in person allowed me to see all sizes and shapes of regular people daring to try something very hard. It opened the door to a world I didn't know existed. First you **SEE** it, then **BELIEVE** it, then **DO** it. This was my "see it" experience.*

# MY ENDURANCE EVENT

*To maintain positive momentum, we can apply newfound confidence to other areas of our lives.*

After watching an Ironman in person, I had a new perspective about challenging perceived athletic limitations. Some people participating in the Ironman did not look like what I expected to see on an endurance course. It stunned my athletic side and I admired those who had the courage to participate. For a very short moment I wished I enjoyed running and could swim, but that wish left my mind as quickly as it arrived. I was happy I enjoyed cycling and looked forward to testing my limits within that sport. There were plenty of long distance rides that would challenge me.

I learned to enjoy cycling during nursing school; it was a stress reliever. I thought I was a natural mountain biker and would not enjoy the mundane boredom of biking on pavement, but I learned quickly I was wrong. My friends took me on fun rides, taught me the etiquette of road cycling and I was hooked. I finished a 100 mile century ride and knew I wanted more. That's when I learned about Lotoja, a one day, 206 mile bike ride from Logan, Utah, to Jackson Hole, Wyoming, and decided I would make that my challenging goal.

There is something about being on a bike that makes me feel like part of my environment, rather than just passing through. There is time to notice the beauty on both sides of the road, especially when riding in the canyons. There is also a sense of achievement, as accomplishments build upon each other and I discover I am able to do things which previously seemed impossible.

As I continued cycling, I felt my body adjust to the new exercise and I could enjoy eating Costco muffins during nursing shifts, without as much guilt. I went for longer and longer rides to help my body get accustomed to being in the seat. I really pushed myself while training because I wanted to give Lotoja my best effort. When I successfully climbed two canyons back-to-back, I shed tears of accomplishment because I didn't know if I could finish that ride. Slowly increasing the challenge built a foundation that allowed me to confidently pursue my ultimate goal.

As the day of Lotoja arrived, my desire to do my best consumed me. I had done all I could to prepare for the challenges ahead and recognized that the hardest athletic event I had participated in was staring me in the face. As I rolled to the start line I felt tears fill my eyes and knew I was ready to be on my way.

My Aunt lives along the course and some of my family traveled to be there to cheer me on as I passed by. Just over an hour after starting, I saw a group of people ahead and knew it was in front of my Aunt's house. As soon as I thought they might be able to see me, I started waving both my arms above my head until I saw some movement within the group and knew they had seen me.

My heart rate jumped as the adrenaline shot through my body. Some of my family had driven a long time in the early morning hours to cheer me on. I could hear their noise as we got closer and it gave me goosebumps! They were waving and cheering frantically. The boost of energy from them was more than what I had anticipated feeling. It was wonderful!! This was my first experience being an athlete trying to accomplish something challenging and having loved ones cheering for me along the way. I've not experienced a similar feeling in my life. It is a literal boost of energy that makes very difficult moments seem feasible.

I made my way over the three mountain passes within the first 107 miles and then prepared to face the notorious winds of the next section. I had done what I could to train for this and made it through that windy section without taking much of a beating. I felt accomplished by being able to ride strongly through those difficult miles.

I was at mile 160 and had the beautiful canyon ahead of me. I quickly realized these may be the hardest miles yet. You see, during my training I made the mistake of assuming if I made it to this point, I would find a way to get to the finish and didn't have any specific goals for these last miles. That was not a smart plan and I paid the price for it. Those last miles took forever, regardless of how beautiful the river or canyon rocks surrounding it were. I inched my way up that canyon like a turtle, and probably looked like one too, leaning over the front of my bike with my tongue hanging out.

Thankfully I reached the end of the canyon and could almost smell the finish, only 15 miles away. I saw my first glimpse of the Tetons and they looked wonderful! Their towering appearance gave me a burst of energy and my pace quickened. Those peaks were a sight for my sore, tired body.

I finally made the last turn and felt a surge of humility and thankfulness. I took a moment to internalize my feelings; I was able to train for, start and about to finish a very hard ride and I did not take that for granted. I felt quite peaceful, alone with my thoughts, until a gust of wind reminded me that I was still on my bike and needed to be present in that moment. I saw a yellow sign ahead and could hardly wait to get close enough to read it. Finally, I read 5 kilometers to go and I didn't know what to think. I kept pedaling and noticed riders were passing me. I didn't care. There was not one competitive desire in my body. My goal was to finish and I knew it was going to happen; I could hardly contain my excitement.

I saw cars being directed off the road and then I saw the 1 km sign followed by orange cones directing us to the other side of the road. Oh my, I could see what might be the finish banner. Was this really happening? Was I actually finishing Lotoja or was this just another attempt to visualize it? Riders were still passing me. Did I want to position myself to cross alone? Hell no, I wanted to get across that line as soon as possible. The line of spectators was closing in quite quickly. Where would my family be? I could hear the cheering and kept pedaling towards the finish. I crossed a timing device and heard someone say "5820 – Finish" and saw the finish banner directly ahead of me. I stopped pedaling, naturally lifted both arms into the air and officially finished Lotoja.

I heard my family going crazy just after the finish banner. I smiled at them and immediately found myself being guided down a chute of volunteers. One of them congratulated me and put a finisher medal into my pocket. I happily got off my bike and walked towards my family coming to celebrate with me. I was thrilled to be engulfed with Jones-esque celebration; there were hugs-a-plenty. I was exhausted and happy to be off my bike. My summer of training was worth it, as I made it across the finish line of a 206 mile bike ride.

> ***Living without Limits:*** *When we challenge ourselves with goals requiring us to stretch beyond previous accomplishments, we become more sensitive to our true potential. Accomplishing hard things requires preparation, a realistic understanding of what will be required of us and a willingness to put forth the effort. And, whether we accomplish our goal or fall short because of things outside of our control, most growth comes during the preparation. Remember we do hard things!*

# RUNNING FOR FUN

*We must recognize when we let things become so big in
our heads that they limit what we think we are able to do.
There are realistic limitations, but it's the unrealistic ones
that are malignant to our potential.*

I learned to appreciate the benefits of exercising while training for Lotoja and, honestly, I still wanted to enjoy my Costco muffins while working, so I needed to come up with a goal to encourage continued exercise. My occasional memory of what I felt during the Ironman, led me to wonder if I could run a marathon. If we think we won't like something, sometimes we're right, sometimes we're not, but there is only one way to find out; I quietly registered to run a local marathon which would keep me exercising through the winter months.

I had never simply run for the fun of it; there was always a goal, homebase or brothers chasing me to create motivation to run. I had to learn about running in its most simple form, as well as the long distance piece of it. I told a few friends about my marathon goal, because they would most assuredly wonder what was happening if I started running. It would be a legitimate concern for them to wonder what was happening to the real Andi, after all, I had never hesitated sharing my dislike of the sport.

I vividly remember my first attempt to run. I was walking my dogs and decided to run a block then walk a block, then run, walk, etc. I was surprised by how out of breath I got in such a short period of time. I instantly questioned my marathon goal, but then brushed those doubts aside and replaced them with thoughts of how great a challenge this would be.

We each have a unique body shape and mine was not created for running. I am blessed to carry my excess muffin storage on my hips and gluteus area. This created a new, uncomfortable sensation as I started running. It literally felt like my rear end was going to bounce off as I ran. I needed a bum bra. I would occasionally look to see if anyone was behind me because nobody needed to see what I imagined was happening back there. There was only one way to remedy this uncomfortable feeling, keep running until all the nerves in that area were damaged and quit communicating with my brain. Some may have suggested reducing my muffin intake, but that was not an option.

When the weather got uncomfortably cold and snowy, I finally purchased a gym pass. I had been able to avoid the boredom associated with treadmill running, but now it was staring me in the face. My first run on the treadmill wasn't as bad as I thought it would be because there were televisions and people exercising in the weight room to provide a bit of distraction. The boredom I dreaded did not hit me until I did my first long run.

My long run taught me about my brain's limit of pretending it was somewhere else, when all my senses were sending information that I was running and running and going nowhere. Gym rats came and went and I was still running in the same place. I was so happy when that run was finished and realized I would do all I could to run outside whenever possible.

As my training marched on, my regular routes became almost as boring as the treadmill. I had to get creative and break free from my close-to-home-running-zone. I discovered destination training runs; I ran to the airport from my house and caught a ride home with my partner returning from a business trip; I ran up a couple of the canyons and arranged a pick-up towards the top; I ran through downtown Salt Lake, although the stoplights made me reconsider doing that one again; I ran to where my brother lived, met him for lunch and then he brought me home. Destination running helped me mentally survive until marathon day.

My marathon day finally arrived. No more training runs, this was the real thing. My cheering crew and I headed out to start our day. There was an inspirational gospel choir singing from atop a bridge above the start line. It was the perfect type of music to get me ready for the day.

I was happy to have some time alone to mentally prepare. I reviewed my plan and reminded myself to be aware of my pace from the beginning. I looked around at my fellow marathoners and took in the moment. So many were already focused on whatever their earphones were feeding their minds; I was reminded I was part of the minority, runners without music in their ears. I felt comfortable with my thoughts and wanted to be interactive and attentive to them during my first marathon.

I made my way to an opening within the crowd to wait for the official start. The choir sang the National Anthem and soon afterwards the countdown started… 5, 4, 3, 2, 1, GO! There was no gun, boom or anything, just GO!

A surge of emotion exploded within my body. My first marathon was officially under way, but I was standing still. I was surrounded by hundreds of runners, eagerly waiting to move forward, encircled by a palpable, nervous energy wanting to run. Twice there was a false start of jogging that ended abruptly.

I could sense the start line ahead and when I was under the bridge, I stepped across the starting mat. I wanted to increase my pace, to even start to jog, but I couldn't. Athletes were maneuvering their way through the group, trying to help themselves go faster, but it wasn't working. I walked along, hoping the pace would increase and it finally did. I felt like my marathon had finally started. Would my training be enough to get me to the finish line? Would my body hold up? Would I see my friends and family along the way? I confidently knew the answer was undoubtedly YES to all the questions zipping around in my head.

Spectators lined the course, anxiously awaiting their loved ones. I knew where my family and friends were planning to see me and I couldn't wait to get there. The crowd of runners started to thin a bit, but the mass of athletes was still affecting my ability to relax and get into a groove. I could see the intersection ahead and knew this was where some of my family would be. I approached a group of people, but there were no familiar faces. I was sad for a moment and realized I had probably missed them on this first sighting. Oh well. Right about then, I saw more people on the side of the road and there was potential this was my family. Yes, it was! I started waving my arm and they finally saw me and waved and cheered. I had seen my first fans and their energy felt great. If this was how it felt every time I saw them, I knew I would be able to finish this marathon.

The miles trudged along and I was happy to have small, achievable goals to focus on. During the first thirteen miles, I saw my family often enough to feel their energy, but also had time to work through challenges on my own. The second thirteen miles were a different story and I didn't expect to see them much at all. Around mile 18, I started to be more aware of how tired I felt and had thoughts of wanting to be done; thankfully there was a surprise ahead.

I was trying to get my mind somewhere else and noticed a spectator in the shade holding the hand of a young child. As I approached her I thought it might be someone who worked in healthcare because she was wearing scrubs. In the split second these thoughts were processing in my head, she looked towards me and I recognized it was my sister-in-law. I started waving and she hollered out to someone else. All of a sudden, a man jumped up from sitting on the lawn and ran towards me. It was my brother, Curtis, whom I had not anticipated would be able to be there. He told me he needed to high-five his sister and caught up alongside me to slap my hand. It was absolutely wonderful to see them. I continued on my way, smiling because of the support I felt from my family. I needed to see someone right then and they were there for me.

When I completed my twenty-first mile, I ventured into unknown territory and those last few miles were as difficult as I heard they would be. I found myself focusing on wanting to be done, which was only making things seem longer and harder. I decided it was time to have a talk with myself about being positive and using my mental strength in positive ways. My positive mind suggested I find things in the environment to help create small, doable goals. I decided to give it a try. I started finding something ahead to focus on, then running until I made it to that item, then finding something else to run towards. This seemed to work and I did my best to stay in the moment.

The other way I passed time was to encourage fellow runners as I passed them. I hoped the athletes appreciated my encouraging comments, because most of them didn't say anything – probably because they were tired and focusing on finishing their marathon. It was fun to have enough energy to be able to do this. It was also a good way to get the focus away from my own discomfort.

I knew we had a few more turns before heading towards the finish and I was getting closer with each step. I was extremely ready to be done running, so I just kept going as fast as possible. I knew there would be some adrenaline for me to finish that last stretch; I just had to get there.

Soon after that, I heard a familiar voice yell my nickname that is used by very few, so it had to be my brother, Greg. I looked and saw Greg and his son fiercely cheering for me. They both looked so excited. As I ran by, he told me to look up and to my left and then took off running. I wondered what they were up to and then I realized this was the part of the marathon I had been envisioning for months. My finish must be just ahead. A surge of adrenaline filled my body and an explosion of emotions headed towards any outlet they could find. I knew the approach to the finish line lay around the next corner. Soon enough, what I had only been able to imagine, would become a reality and I could hardly wait!

There was fencing along the roadway, but there were hardly any spectators behind it anymore. It was kind of sad. I remembered Greg telling me to look up and then figured what he meant. There were walkways crossing above the road. I looked up and saw Greg and his kids all cheering loudly for me. I waved and spread my arms like a plane and zig-zagged my way along that final approach. The excitement of being at the end carried me through that moment. I saw the finish banner ahead and felt a wave of amazement pass over me; I was actually just about to finish a marathon. Wow, all my questions about what a marathon felt like were being answered.

The sound of spectators cheering was wonderful. I approached another walkway above me and looked up to see my entire family waving their arms and cheering so loudly. I gave them a huge smile and a big happy wave. Another surge of energy helped me start sprinting and it felt awesome for my feet to fly underneath me and cross the finish line.

Someone handed me a finisher's medal and I continued walking down the chute. It felt good to not have to run. I saw my family making their way to a place we could meet, so I headed that direction.

The area finally cleared out of athletes and there was an opening for me to get to my family and friends. I gave so many hugs, with my salty face and everything. Someone handed me my flip flops, so I put them on and my feet were overwhelmed with happiness to be out of my running shoes. I was a marathon finisher!

> ***Living without Limits:*** *My body was not built to be comfortable while running. If I would have chosen to remain comfortable, I would have never learned what existed beyond it. Running taught me that reaching beyond comfortable can bring rewards beyond understanding.*

# IRONMAN THOUGHTS

*Our biggest dreams always start as a simple thought; what those thoughts become depends upon how they are nurtured.*

Some significant things happened in my life during a relatively short period of time that guided me to gather the courage to participate in an event that would indeed challenge my perceived limits.

- I personally witnessed regular people participating in an Ironman
- I trained for and finished a 206 mile bike ride
- I registered for, trained for and finished a marathon
- I watched the inspirational broadcast of the Ironman in Hawaii
- Ironman Arizona changed their race from April to November

I watched the broadcast of the Ironman in Hawaii and noticed how differently I felt after personally interacting with athletes on an Ironman course. Those athletes were inspiring, regardless of whether they finished their race or not, they seemed like regular people who happened to have the courage to chase their dreams.

Ironman races are lifetime goals for all types of people and if you choose to participate, you must register well in advance, sometimes even one full year ahead of the event. This takes a special type of dedication, one that seemed insurmountable to me. Insurmountable until I remembered my recent courageous decision to go to nursing school. If I could do that, why not put that same dedication and commitment towards trying to finish an Ironman.

While watching the Ironman broadcast, I heard the announcement that Ironman Arizona was changing its typical early spring competition to late autumn. If I was to do an Ironman, that one would be the most practical. I looked it up online and saw that registration was currently open for the November race. Oh my!

Before I knew it I was sitting in front of my computer, easily marching through the steps of registration until I got to the Submit button. I paused emphatically, recognizing and respecting what it would mean if I clicked that button. Thankfully I found the courage to follow through and just did it, I clicked that one simple click and BELIEVED I could do it.

It wasn't an easy decision to register. Actually, as I reflect upon the many challenges contained within an Ironman, one of the hardest was the decision to realistically consider it and then actually click the registration button. It took me some time to let my decision to register settle before I could share it with others. I anticipated the question of why and didn't have an easy answer. I had seen the variety of athletes on the Coeur D'Alene course and knew I fell somewhere in the middle; I had recently watched the Hawaii broadcast and wanted to feel what it was like to push beyond my limits; and the timing seemed to be right to take on such an adventure. I guess my answer was a question: why not give it a try?

My Ironman news traveled quickly. I learned that my brother, Greg, wanted to do it with me. I was stunned. Most people don't decide to do an Ironman because someone they care about, and maybe feel a bit protective of, decided to do one, but Greg isn't like most people. He wanted to do the Ironman with me, not because he wanted to challenge himself, but because he wanted to be by my side. He found a way to register for Ironman Arizona and become another Jones taking on this challenge.

Now, how in the world does someone start training for an Ironman? I figured I had better conquer the swim first. Luckily the gym I belonged to had a pool, so I bought some goggles and a swim cap and headed to the water. It was January, but the pool was still full of people. I wondered why so many people were swimming in the winter, but I learned I would be entering a new world as I trained for this challenge.

I found a lane where nobody was swimming and cautiously lowered my white body, with its muffin behind into the water. I looked across the 25 foot length, pushed off the wall and headed to the other side. I vividly remember feeling like I had swallowed the entire pool by the time I got across my lane and I could hardly breathe! I hung onto the edge of the pool and realized I had made a horrible mistake by thinking I could do any event that included swimming. I was dumbfounded and wondered what I was going to do. I let my initial panic relax and opened myself for the huge dose of humility descending upon me. I wanted to run away from that water, but I calmly convinced myself to stay there and proceeded to turn around and swim back to where I had started. There was no miraculous reduction of the amount of water I swallowed, or the exertion I felt as I finally made it to the other side, but I did keep my mind under control and avoided additional panic. I slowly made my way back and forth for a few minutes and then let myself leave the water.

I processed my first swimming experience and thankfully remembered I had a friend who may be able to help me. I shared with her what happened when I tried to swim and she immediately said she could help. The next day I found myself in the pool with her, learning what I needed to do to survive my attempt to swim efficiently. She provided some key concepts that would hopefully allow me to continue pursuing my goal of starting an Ironman, let alone finishing one. I could now work on swimming without feeling like I was drinking the pool, or becoming exhausted in such a short time.

I proceeded to diligently swim three to four times each week, which meant being at the gym when the doors opened at 5:00 a.m., so I could swim before work. That was difficult to get used to. I commuted to work by bike, so I was already cycling regularly and I ran three to four times each week, mostly on the treadmill until winter thankfully turned to spring and I could run outdoors. As my training increased, it required the time of a part-time job, which made it quite challenging sometimes. I took my training seriously because I wanted to do all I could to get across that Ironman finish line.

> ***Living without Limits:*** *The process of working towards our event or goal is where strength of character is created. Following through with the little challenges during preparation can be the hardest. It's easier to keep going on race day because that is our big moment; finding the determination and commitment to get up early on cold, wet training days is what strengthens our foundation and, ultimately, determines how much we struggle during the process of achieving our goal.*

# UNEXPECTED CHALLENGE

*Things can always get harder! Sometimes the road seems so straight, until something jumps out and changes everything.*

My training for Ironman Arizona was on track and I felt better prepared each week. I should have known some sort of challenge was around the corner. I was riding to work in late September and decided to head up the canyon instead of riding straight to work. If I rode up the canyon before work, I wouldn't have to train as long that evening. I left the house at my normal time of 6:00 a.m., which means it was still on the darker side, and the bike I was riding didn't have lights because I seldom ride it when it is dark. Can you guess where this is headed?

I was headed up the canyon, about four miles from my house, when I saw headlights from a car shine on something I thought was a loose, dangling spider web in front of me. I leaned my head to the side, to miss getting that web in my face and something smacked me hard enough to knock me off my bike. I was stunned and hoped nobody had seen me run head on into a large, black garbage can waiting to be emptied. I picked myself up, straightened my bike and tried to process what happened. What was I thinking, riding without a light on my bike when it was dark outside?

I noticed my finger felt like it was jammed. I tugged on it, like I did after jamming fingers while playing basketball, which appeared to help. I walked my bike to the other side of the road and it seemed to be working alright, so I got on and started coasting down the canyon. The skies started to lighten and I found myself realizing how stupid I had been. I was lucky to not have been seriously hurt. I slowly made my way to work and figured I would deal with my training ride after work.

I went into the conference room where my manager and another nurse were chatting. I had not changed into my scrubs yet, so they wondered what was up and asked how I was doing. I shared my stupid decision and showed them my hand, hoping they would confirm I did not need to do anything since I could move all my fingers. That's not what happened; they both suggested I go to the emergency room and get an x-ray. I had to trust my experienced nurse friends and reluctantly went to get my hand x-rayed.

Shortly after my x-ray, the doctor came back with unexpected news, I had broken my hand. I immediately told her this couldn't happen because I was training for an Ironman! She was genuinely sorry for me, but what could she do. I found myself in a situation I had never been in before. I fiercely needed to escape the disappointment I felt; this couldn't be true! What had I done? A broken hand because I was stupid enough to ride up the canyon before dawn, without lights on my bike!

The doctor told me they would not know if the fracture was surgical until next week. I was still processing the first piece of devastating information, but knew it was not good for my Ironman hopes to delay any procedure. I sat in silence as they splinted my hand and told me to come back next week.

The next day I felt alright and went to work. I knew I would face questions of what happened and the truth would be embarrassing so, since I had been riding in the mountains, surrounded by unseen moose and deer, why couldn't I say I hit one of them? With this thought in the back of my head, I found myself sharing an alternate version of what happened: in the morning darkness, I rode into something big and black, which turned out to be a moose. The reaction of my coworkers was priceless and I knew this would be my story. Why not have some fun surrounding my stupidity? I wonder how many still think I hit a moose.

While at work, I got a call from another surgery center that happened to have had a cancellation and, if I could come in for an appointment within the hour, they could see me and do any needed surgery the next day. I had to jump on that opportunity, as I had limited time before my Ironman. My manager covered for me and I went to the appointment.

Indeed my hand needed surgery and they scheduled me for the next day. What a mini miracle that was. Somehow my non-emergent hand fracture had been surgically repaired within 60 hours of my ill-fated encounter with the "moose".

I shared my Ironman goal with my surgeon and he supported my desire to still participate. He asked that I keep my hand dry and only ride indoors. I could run, as long as I stopped if it hurt. I would only be able to run or ride indoors for the next couple of weeks. This was all fine, because at least I was still able to work towards my Ironman goal, which I had thought was gone because of one stupid, stupid decision. That was so close!

I have never experienced the emotion involved with having something taken away that I'd been working so diligently towards. I was a mental and emotional mess as I struggled with the possibility of my goal not being possible. I was lost, silently frustrated and not in control of what I could do. I was only able to run short bits, with my arm elevated to avoid blood throbbing pain, but no swimming or outdoor bike riding during those first two weeks. Not the distances in my training plan for an Ironman only six weeks away.

I couldn't handle staying out of the water, so one week after surgery, I bargained with myself and found a way to get in the water while still adhering to my limitations. I rested my healing hand on a kickboard and only swam using my left arm. It felt wonderful to get in the water, but I only lasted a few minutes. I felt much better afterwards and was content to wait another week, when I would be able to submerge my surgically repaired hand in the water and try to swim normally.

I could finally ride my bike outside and jumped for joy. I felt invincible and headed out for a long ride which definitely pushed me too far, too soon. I realized I was not doing well after already riding to the turn-around point, which meant there were 45 miles remaining to make it home.

I had not considered my body position would be different on my bike because I could not hold onto anything with my hand. I found myself exhausted, both physically and mentally. I remember being behind my friend and struggling to keep her in sight. My back hurt, my neck didn't want to support my head any longer and my shoulder was angry at my hand for not being able to help balance my weight. I limped home and asked my body to forgive me for pushing it too hard. I had never ridden with a handicap and had no idea how hard it would be. I learned I was not superhuman and needed to listen to my body as it healed, otherwise I may cause further damage. I had a new normal and I needed to learn to work within it.

This experience sufficiently humbled me, both physically and mentally. I have never been challenged in that way. Up until my encounter with the "moose", I was in control of everything; of how much I trained, of when I trained and I was able to do all I needed to feel prepared to achieve my goal. When I broke my hand, I lost the freedom of being able to train as I needed and, instead, had to train to the level that my injury allowed. I was at the mercy of my hand. This thoroughly destroyed my confidence and I realized that I may not be able to participate in Ironman Arizona.

I had just enough time before Ironman day to gather the broken pieces of my confidence and find a way to build it back, to a new, stronger confidence. I incorporated this unexpected challenge of competing with an injury into my race day expectations and relied on the knowledge that many athletes would be participating with some sort of injury and we would do our best to find a way to finish. My injury would not keep me from starting the race, but I was aware of the reality that it could keep me from finishing it.

> ***Living without Limits:*** *We never know what our future may entail. I take each day for what it is and am thankful for what I have that day because it will eventually change. It is my responsibility to live my life without regrets and make adjustments as needed to be happy with what I have. Those who choose to focus on what they don't have, or*

*allow negativity to overpower their day, are in risk of missing opportunities of the moment.*

# IRONMAN ARIZONA

*THINK it, BELIEVE it, PREPARE for it, then give all you have to DO it!*

It was finally time to put all my training to the test on the Ironman Arizona course. As I arrived in Tempe, I saw the course and that first glimpse of the water was surprisingly emotional. I saw the swim buoys and felt chills spread throughout my body as tears filled my eyes. The chills quickly turned to a dreaded feeling and I had to look away. The swim was my unknown and I did not want to deal with it yet.

I checked in, which confirmed I was actually registered for this Ironman. It was no longer a dream, it was reality. I walked to the water and was humbled. I knew the swim would take courage and I believed I could do it. I didn't allow my thoughts to go much further than that because it would not have been good. I was very quiet, within myself and my thoughts, even though there were people all around.

We met for a practice swim on the actual course. It was a cool morning with the sun still low in the sky. We got into our wetsuits, I taped my still healing fingers and we made our way to the stairs leading into the water. There I was, trying to process that my next step would put me into the actual swim course, oh my! The athlete in front of us got right in, Greg fell in because he thought there was another step, and I cautiously let myself down into the Ironman Arizona swim course, doing my best to stay positive.

Our practice swim was just OK. My goggles were hard to see out of and the wind was creating a current against us. The waves slapped me in the face and tossed me around, which I didn't like at all. We stayed together and kept swimming to short landmarks: first the bridge, then the buoy, things like that. I tried to find a positive mental place to go to while I was in the water, but it wasn't happening. I was ready to head back. We made our way back and somehow got ourselves up those stairs and out of the water. I didn't feel much better after swimming, which was not what I had hoped for.

Race day quickly arrived and I got up, got myself ready and waited for the others. Practically all of my family had found a way to be there to support both Greg and myself. It was going to be a day to remember. I reviewed my Ironman notes and knew I was as ready as I would ever be. It was time to face whatever lay ahead.

We got our race numbers written on our arms and then heard the announcer tell us we should be making our way to the swim entrance. It is never fun to put a wetsuit on, but I happily squeezed myself into mine, because this was my big day. We hugged our family and squeezed through the hundreds of spectators to make our way into the transition area.

The announcer was well into his inspirational monologue. I looked around and we were surrounded by hundreds of athletes who looked exactly like us, in wetsuits and blue or pink swim caps. The energy was palpable; nerves were out of control; we were slowly being drawn towards the Ironman swim archway. There were a few smiles, but most of us were looking straight forward, preparing for what lay ahead. Greg was constantly rubbing his arms and trying to loosen up, while I was mentally preparing to jump in the water. At one point I threw my arms around Greg and was so relieved he was with me. He knew this was my hard part and did his best to give me confidence, even though his nerves were going crazy themselves. He had his own concerns, but right then he was there for me and I was thankful.

We were still moving forward, at a slow, constant pace, as if we were unknowingly being drawn towards the water. I looked at my watch and saw we had eight minutes before the cannon would sound for us. We needed to get in the water; there was not time to wait to walk through the gate leading to the water. Athletes started to climb over the railing and make their way over some narrow framing and jump in from there. This is where Greg and I got in the water. I remember him turning to me and telling me that this one was for both of us and that he loved me. I told him I loved him too. I could feel tears welling up in my eyes, but quickly gathered myself, as it would not be good to start the day with moisture inside my goggles.

Before I knew it, Greg was climbing over the railing and turned to make sure I could safely do the same. I followed and watched him balance out to the water and jump in. Then, as if I was on autopilot, I did exactly the same. There was little thought process involved; I just did it. Whew, the first hard thing could be checked off my mental list. I was in the water, surrounded by hundreds of athletes.

We made our way together, towards the start, until Greg disappeared into the mix of swim caps. We were on our own, but it was alright.

I looked at my fellow athletes, staying afloat in the water, and could see reflections of what I was feeling on their faces; so many emotions were written on them. The water was cool and I was getting used to it. I looked up and saw spectators cheering from the bridge above. A long day was awaiting us all, both spectators and athletes. I thought of my family on the sidelines and remembered what it was like watching the swim of Ironman Coeur D'Alene; I wondered if Arizona would feel similar.

I heard the announcer say, "I have one last thing to say to all you athletes out there. By the end of today, you WILL be an Ironman!" Then, before the goose bumps could make their way to the surface of my body, there was a loud BOOM and we were off. The spectators went crazy and we slowly started swimming forward. That moment will be etched in my mind's eye forever because it is when I transitioned from completing my training to beginning my Ironman experience. What an emotionally exhilarating change of focus!

**Swim:** The swim was exactly how I imagined it would be. There were athletes surrounding me and with almost every stroke I was hit or kicked by someone or the one hitting or kicking someone else. There were a few times I stopped because I hit someone and got off balance, but for the most part I was able to keep moving forward, even with the contact. Occasionally I would be next to an athlete, swimming the same pace, and realize we were looking at each other. It was an interesting distraction for that short second.

As I looked ahead, I could see the big red turn buoy and it seemed really far away. I was swimming straight and could not wait to be able to turn around. When I reached it, I was disappointed to see there was another big red buoy to the north that we needed to swim towards before we actually turned around. I mistakenly thought I would be able to turn around at that first buoy. Damn!

It felt great to turn around at that second buoy and know I was headed back. I got into a nice rhythm and was able to relax and breathe rhythmically. I felt like I was in the pool and was able to focus on keeping my head down, taking long strokes and rotating my shoulders and hips. I even casually looked at the volunteers on surfboards, kayaks and other watercrafts as I swam by. This was a nice time of the swim, until I hit another athlete, which dissolved my relaxed rhythm and shocked me back into the reality of where I was.

An athlete was right next to me and not swimming straight. He would veer into me and then away from me. I tried to speed up and swim away from him, but it didn't work. As I look back at that experience, I realize it was probably me doing the veering and I was the one bothering him. I am a special athlete who swims a zig zag pattern when approaching the end of my swim.

Before I knew it I was swimming under the bridge where we started our swim. I was very aware of the big, concrete supports as I made my way under the bridge and stayed far away from them, as I did not want to hit them. That would leave a mark. As I made my final turn and headed down the homestretch, my body filled with a sense of accomplishment and I knew I was going to make it.

I swam to the stairs and graciously accepted help out of the water. My feet found solid ground and happily made their way up the stairs and out of that water. I had officially finished the swim and could not wait to get on my bike and further internalize what I had already accomplished.

I was about to experience how volunteers directly help athletes during endurance events. I had wriggled one arm out of the wet, tight constricting device I had squeezed myself into earlier that morning, but I needed help with the rest. Wetsuit strippers were there and easily slid my other arm out, told me to sit on the ground, and in one smooth motion, my wetsuit was off and I was on my way. I could not have done that alone without it becoming a purely comical performance.

On my way to the changing tent, I heard my name being yelled and looked to see two of my brothers in their neon green shirts. It was wonderful to see them so quickly after my swim. I continued forward and shortly thereafter saw the remainder of my green shirted family members cheering wildly for me. I felt my smile burst through and happily waved as I passed them. It felt wonderful to have my family there for me and be rejuvenated by their energy.

I made my way into the change tent with my bag of things for my ride. Almost immediately a volunteer asked if she could help. I didn't really know how she would help me, but I happily accepted it. She politely asked if she could empty my bag and, after the contents were lying in front of me, she went into action.

She handed me my towel so I could dry my feet as she reached around me and put my race belt on. I wanted to wipe my face with the towel, but she took it from me, saying there were allergens from the ground on it. She carefully found a dry, clean corner and I used that part to dry my face. She was so meticulous and thoughtful. Before I knew it my socks were resting on my knees, waiting to be put on, my shoes were undone and opened wide to ease entry of my feet, my food was in my pockets and she asked what else she could do. I asked for help taking the tape off my injured fingers, which initiated her question, wondering if it was some type of swimming strategy. I smiled and shared my encounter with the "moose" a few weeks ago. She chuckled.

My volunteer wished me a great race and I very sincerely thanked her for helping me. I didn't have to think of anything during my transition, she literally took care of everything. She was awesome and helped me in the best way possible.

I found my bike and headed towards the exit. We coasted through the spectator packed "no-pass zone", and it was hard to ride slowly because my legs desperately wanted to get going. I heard intense screaming of my name and looked to see my crazed, green-shirted, family members cheering wildly. It was invigorating to see them and know they would be there during my entire adventure.

**Bike:** I was finally on the open road and it felt wonderful. I settled into my bike and found myself passing riders and also being passed by some amazing athletes. I was happy to notice Greg at the beginning of his first loop. I saw him too late to say anything, but at least I knew he was on his bike and he looked strong. I saw him again while finishing my second loop and yelled to him so he would see me; he appeared very relieved and I later found out he was worried I had not finished the swim because he hadn't seen me. I should have expected that from my worry prone brother.

I was approaching my family and could see they were all looking away from me. They were going to miss seeing me if they kept looking that direction. One of them looked my way so I started waving my arm in the air. They recognized me and I heard them say, "Here she is", and everyone turned around as I was literally right next to them. I waved as they cheered and was quickly on my way.

I finished my second loop and was excited to start the last one. My family saw me coming this time and we exchanged smiles as I passed. I happily held up my index finger up to represent I only had one loop left. They were again loud and energetic. I was energized and ready to give this final lap my best so off I went.

I was riding a good, strong pace and had not been affected by my healing hand. In fact, I had hardly noticed my taped fingers. I was doing as well as I possibly could, just as I had visualized.

I maneuvered my bike through all the turns for the last time and was happy to ride straight into the transition zone instead of turning to start another loop. It was nice to slow down, cautiously make my way through the "no passing zone" and prepare to get off my bike. There were more crazy green-shirted fans screaming for me as I got off my bike and headed to get my run bag. My family was so encouraging to see and hear along the way. Their support made my smile even bigger.

I got off my bike, handed it to the nice volunteer and made my way to the transition area. My legs felt secure under me, which was nice. I got my run bag and headed towards the change tent, where another volunteer asked if she could help me. Again, my entire transition went smoothly. My volunteer helped me and I thanked her as I headed out to start my marathon.

**Run:** It was great to see my family smiling and give them high fives. I was starting my third sport and closing in on unknown obstacles. My swim and bike training had been sufficient, now to see about my run training. Thankfully, my heart and mind felt ready for whatever was ahead; the yet unknown lay within everything else.

I quickly came upon the first aid station and walked through it, as my plan was to walk through each one. I took a glass of ice water and poured it over my head. It was cold and my face must have shown the shock because I noticed an older gentleman smile who was sitting nearby. He told me to remember how it felt to jump in the cool water earlier that morning. I smiled with him and went on my way.

A little while after the aid station, the hint of a challenge showed its sneaky face. My stomach felt tender, like muscle soreness with a hint of nausea. It could be a long marathon if this kept up. I thought carefully about what might be happening and what I could do about it. I decided to be really careful about the food I ate.

I saw the one mile marker and was happy to leave it in the dust; one mile done, twenty-five to go. I approached another aid station and a volunteer told me how great I looked, that my pace was perfect. I was surprised by his direct interaction with me and appreciated it. I got something to drink and ate part of a banana; I was careful while still trying to figure out what was happening with my stomach.

During Ironman check in, spectators can submit written messages for their athlete which would be broadcasted on a big sign during the motivational mile. Our motivational mile was around mile 8, after a long, boring section running through a parking lot. I crossed an electronic device which triggered my message to scroll across the big sign; it read, "A. Jones #2394

– You are awesome!" It was a great distraction for me, especially after struggling with boredom during the previous few miles.

The terrain thankfully changed and we were able to run across some bridges. I enjoyed running across one in particular because there were spectators reading our names off our bib numbers and cheering for us by name. This always made me smile and I thanked them. Never underestimate the encouragement athletes gain from interacting with spectators, especially when calling us by name.

I was nearing where my family would probably be and, at the bottom of a grassy trail, I saw my dad with his camera pointed my direction. I waved and smiled and was very happy to see him. I turned the corner and immediately saw my big group of greenies, cheering wildly for me. They were absolutely awesome! I smiled and gave everyone I could high fives. I enjoyed seeing their individual faces and smiling with each one of them; it was hard to do that while on my bike because I was going too fast, so I took some time to enjoy my interactions with them. I could not imagine being on the course without them cheering me on. The other spectators were great, but encouragement from my family always felt stronger and had a direct pathway to my heart.

I started my second loop and was pleasantly surprised with the pace I had been able to maintain during my first loop. I found my thoughts wandering towards giving myself permission to slow down because I could still finish with a respectable time, even if I walked more. I immediately remembered some advice about never giving up on your goals, especially during the marathon. This applied to me at that exact moment. I had worked and trained to be able to achieve my goals and, to change the parameters of what was acceptable, would be giving in. I wanted to strive for what I had trained to do, every step of the way. I grabbed hold of that thought and didn't let it go for the remainder of the run. It was exactly what I needed in my head at that point of the race.

My stomach still hurt and my typical foot pain would occasionally scream out for attention. To placate the pain, I would instinctively say "Ouch" and continue running until it went away. I was silently looking forward to stop running, but was determined to focus on one mile at a time, instead of looking at the daunting task ahead. It was the only way to conquer this giant, one small goal at a time.

I had been passing and being passed by the same athlete for quite some time. I couldn't decide if it bugged me or not. During my walk up a steep hill, someone was talking with me so I looked to my side and it was this athlete. He told me I was just like his wife, that I never stopped going. We were the tortoise and the hare. We talked for a bit, until his pace was quicker than mine, so he went ahead. Then, as I passed him on the run down the hill, I said to him, "Here comes the tortoise, passing the hare". He said he was used to it because of his wife. This was a fun distraction while it lasted.

The sun was a beautiful desert sun as it lowered in the horizon. I wondered where I would be on the course when it set and hoped I would have a good view. I could not have planned my position more perfectly; I had the best view possible as it lowered out of sight. It was beautiful and I took a moment to enjoy it. It was energizing in a peaceful way.

Just before starting my third loop, I decided to eat a cookie and oh my, it tasted like it had been delivered straight from heaven. After that I looked forward to eating cookies, but knew I had to be careful with my stomach. I bargained with my mouth and compromised that it would be better to space the cookies over every other aid station, just to be safe. I also had heard that the chicken broth tasted amazingly, so I gave it a try. The saltiness and warmness felt divine after the sun disappeared and temperatures cooled. I alternated cookies and chicken broth at aid stations after that, which gave me a small thing to look forward to, as my race challenges continued.

Around mile 17, I felt a strong sense of light headedness which caught me off guard. I took some deep breaths and further realized how much stress I was putting on my entire body. I slowed down until the oozy feeling went away. I was grateful to be on my last loop. As I neared the area with more spectators, I thought it would help me run more, but even with their motivation, I still had to walk. I decided to keep walking until I felt I could keep running until I saw the finish chute.

That time finally came so I got my engine going and anticipated the sign directing me to the finish. It came into view and I thankfully followed the directions to the finish as beams of happiness prepared to burst from my body.

I judiciously made that last turn and found myself inside the finisher chute surrounded by spectators going crazy. I heard my name over the loud speaker. I felt I was being carried towards the finish line, full of relief that I had made it. My family was on my left, but once my eyes caught sight of the finish arch, I couldn't stop looking at that wonderful sight. The lights were bright, the spectators were incredibly loud and there was a finish banner waiting especially for me. I lifted my arms in the air and ran across the finish line. It was finally OK to stop running. I DID IT!! I was an Ironman Finisher!

After finishing, volunteers quickly got on each side of me, wrapped me in a foil blanket as they congratulated me and tried to determine how I was doing. They asked how I was feeling and I replied that I thought I was doing pretty well. They didn't loosen their support around my shoulders one bit. They led me to get my medal, where we were overpowered by a loud, cheering, crazed sound coming from our left. We looked to see my greenies and they looked so happy. We walked towards them and my volunteers relinquished me to my family's care. I thoroughly appreciated every little thing all volunteers did throughout the day. They treated me as if I was family. I've not experienced an event with such incredible support from volunteers, they were truly inspirational.

There were hugs from everyone as I entered the spectator zone. It was wonderful to be done and be with everyone who had spent the day with me. What an experience!

I knew it would be better to walk around so I slowly made my way into the secured, athlete area to get my warm clothes. It felt peaceful to be alone and able to internalize the feelings surrounding what I just accomplished. As athletes walked by, I congratulated them and they returned the gesture. We knew that we had each spent the day working through challenges and this silent understanding bound us together. It was great to be at the end of our day.

I went back to the finish and found a place on the bleachers to applaud those finishing. I held out my hand for athletes to slap and felt blessed to feel strong enough to cheer for my fellow Ironman finishers. What an experience, it was awesome! We waited for Greg and cheered loudly as he rounded the corner and made his way across the finish.

Everyone has their own issues to deal with after putting their bodies through an Ironman race. My issues healed completely and my pre-race injury helped strengthen me mentally. All things considered, my Ironman Arizona was a success and just as challenging as it should have been. I am an Ironman!

> ***Living without Limits:*** *After all my training and challenges during Ironman day, I can say that one of the hardest things to do within this entire Ironman experience was to make the decision to register. This has helped me in my day-to-day life by knowing that sometimes the*

*hardest thing within doing something challenging is the decision to commit to do it.*

# REACHING FOR A STAR

*If you reach for the stars, don't be surprised if you touch one!*

There was an Ironman world I had no idea existed. I was still absorbing my Ironman Arizona finish when I learned about the lottery for the Ironman World Championship in Hawaii. The most common way to participate in the World Championships is to win your age group at qualifying Ironman events. The other way is by winning a lottery. I chuckled to myself as the silly thought of entering it crossed my mind and then easily let it go.

A couple of months later, I got an email reminding Ironman athletes that the lottery deadline was quickly approaching and to get our names entered. It reminded me of my earlier lottery thoughts and this time I chose to share them with a few friends, but they didn't have much to say. The chances of winning were very slim; thousands of hopeful athletes would enter and it cost a decent amount just to enter. My non-gambling self believed I would be throwing money away, but one friend felt the opposite. She felt it was a once in a lifetime chance and if it was meant to happen, I would be selected, if it wasn't then I could easily let it go. For some reason her words stuck in my mind and I did the crazy thing and entered the Ironman World Championship lottery.

My life went back to normal and I essentially forgot about entering the lottery. The winners would be notified the following Spring, which seemed far away. Fast forward... in early April, I got a call from a triathlon organization asking if I was willing to be interviewed about being a first time Ironman who was a bit older than most rookies. I am not one who likes the spotlight, but maybe my story would be interesting to someone, so I agreed to be interviewed.

I met the reporter at the hospital where I worked because they wanted to interview me on a day I worked. We casually talked about how I got into the sport of triathlon and I shared my story until it was time for the interview to officially start. I quickly realized I was much more comfortable talking casually than being officially interviewed. I tried to relax and be natural, but it was everything except natural for me. I did my best to answer the questions, but overall the interview was difficult and quite uncomfortable.

I could tell he was starting to wrap it up and felt a bit of relief. He asked what was next for me and I told him about my crazy decision to enter the lottery. He asked what it would mean for me to be able to participate in the Hawaii Ironman. This was the easiest question to answer; it came as natural as anything could. I told him it would be incredible. It is the ultimate Ironman and I would be honored to compete alongside such elite athletes. He stood up and said, "Well…" and walked towards the door, reached down to pick something up, then walked back towards me. Time stood still and I had no clue what was happening. He proceeded to tell me that I would be participating in the Hawaii Ironman in October and handed me a large announcement stating that I had won the lottery. I was in total shock. I had NO IDEA this was a setup for winning the lottery. I have never been so surprised and it was caught on camera. I felt tears filling my eyes and could not wipe the stunned smile off my face. My entire body had no idea what to do. I actually won the lottery and would be going to KONA!!

They asked to film me telling someone I knew, so we made our way to the Surgical ICU so I could tell my friend. She happened to walk into the hallway right as we got there. I held up the certificate and shared with her that I had won the Hawaii lottery. She screamed in excitement and gave me a big hug. It was caught on camera and was a spectacularly genuine reaction. It could not have been planned better; it was perfect to be with my friend who was the one who inspired me to enter the lottery.

I said goodbye to the news team and did not know what to do with myself. I realized quickly I would not be able to continue working, so I went home to enjoy the evening and share my incredible news. I hoped to share this experience in a way that would seem like a normal interview with the lottery news at the end, just like I had been surprised. It worked out perfectly.

When I shared my surprise with my partner, there was jumping up and down with flapping arms and screaming, followed by uncontrollable tears. It was a moment of pure excitement, surprise, shock and bewilderment, a once-in-a-lifetime experience to remember forever.

The news aired that night and the story was an awesome three minute synopsis of the last year of my athletic life. As of today, it still lives on you tube entitled "Winning the Ironman Lottery" by Fields Moseley. As expected, the phone rang, and family and friends enthusiastically congratulated me one after another. I was exhausted and my bed was a welcomed escape, although, my mind would not turn off; how could it after a day like that?

The next day my fellow nurses and hospital staff who had seen the news congratulated me. The well wishes continued for weeks. People I did not know would see me in the hallway and say "I saw you on the news – Congratulations!" I could not get away from the public eye. It was nice to have people excited for me, but I found it exhausting to have that part of my life so public. This was only the beginning of sharing a piece of me that I had preferred to keep tucked behind safe walls. It was obviously time for those walls to start coming down.

I was chosen to participate in the Ironman World Championship – the event I remember watching as a young girl and being in awe of what those athletes were able to accomplish. I needed to get busy and renew my gym pass; I had another Ironman to train for.

> ***Living without Limits:*** *It is when we least expect our lives to change direction, that we are the most vulnerable to character building opportunities.*

# LOTTERY HANGOVER

*When we recognize we are engaged in something that will only happen once in our lifetime, we need to give it our all. We usually grow from those experiences at an equitable level of the effort we put towards them.*

Many of us remember watching the broadcast of the Ironman race in Kona, Hawaii. My specific memories are thoughts of how uncomfortable it must be to ride a bike in a swimsuit. I did not understand the grueling length or harsh racing conditions or that it combined endurance distances in each of three different sports. I remember watching two women crawl to get across the finish line and realizing what they were trying to accomplish was obviously a challenge. Little did I know that years later, I would find myself fighting to make it across that same finish line.

It took some time to process that I had won the lottery. I was in denial and it was hard to start training. I was confused and wanted to understand my feelings about Kona; sometimes I felt excited and eager, while other times I was hesitant and overwhelmed. I wanted so badly to embrace the fact I won the lottery and feel positive about the training required, but I was still recovering from Arizona.

A huge part of me felt ungrateful for feeling that way about Kona, but it was my conflict and, ultimately, would become part of my Kona Ironman story. Just like my broken hand became a chapter of Ironman Arizona. It seems that every part of training for and participating in an Ironman is unpredictable and, in the end, the hard times are what mold every part of the athlete who crosses that finish line – mentally, emotionally and physically.

My watch read "125 days till Kona", which made my heart skip a beat. I was able to start thinking about training and have a better attitude about it. During an open water practice swim, I was able to help a co-worker who was experiencing cold, open water swimming for the first time. I talked with her and stayed alongside her in the water, until we made it to shore. She told me I made her feel safe and she was proud I had been selected for Kona. It was an experience I learned from, as just one year ago I was the swimmer on the panicking side of my own cold water swimming experience.

As I finished long training rides followed by long training runs, I visualized them as the end of my run in Kona. I cannot believe how real they were. I would feel my throat tighten up, I got goosebumps and my heart rate increased quickly. I practiced finishing strong at the virtual finish line in front of my house. It always felt great to be done with those tough training days.

Two months before Kona, I participated in a half distance Ironman in Colorado. My swim and bike went well, but I learned an important lesson during my run. I ran well for the first six miles, but then got an abdominal cramp that would not go away. It forced me to walk more than I would have liked to. I also felt blisters developing on my foot. I had been dumping water on my head for the majority of the run, which is known to contribute to foot problems. My final miles were uncomfortable, but I worked through them. I crossed the finish line after a mental, physical and emotional learning experience. It was not easy, not even a little bit, but I found a way to finish with a smile on my face… an awesome Kona training day!

Another training experience taught me why long, hot training days are so important. I finished my long swim and waited for the heat of the day to head out for my ride and run. I looked forward to exposing my body to hot temperatures and gusty winds. I only saw one other cyclist during my ride, which showed that the hot, windy conditions were not preferable. As the miles ticked away, I found myself irritated by things that do not normally bother me. My water was a bit warmer than I like, and the wind seemed to be affecting me more than usual. The miles got longer instead of shorter. I kept plugging away and convinced myself that I did not need to run after my ride because of how hard I was working on my bike. It would be OK if I skipped one run.

I finished my ride and was still very frustrated about needing to run, but knew it would be best if I went. I got myself out the door because I could run through hundreds of football tailgaters as part of my run; they would be a nice distraction. I may not like running, but liking it is not a pre-requisite to participate in an Ironman. In fact, overcoming that type of obstacle adds to the allure of an Ironman.

I finished my run, which included many walking breaks, but I had exercised on tired legs and a frustrated mind. I dragged myself into the shower and then onto the couch. As a second thought, I got on the scale and weighed myself. I was shocked to see I had lost five pounds during my training. It immediately explained why my attitude was unusually negative; I was dehydrated! I needed to drink significantly more water in intensely hot conditions. What a great lesson to learn during training, instead of on race day!

One week later I rode the same ride in hotter conditions, but this time I drank more frequently. I felt totally different mentally and was not as exhausted to start my run. I felt better about my awareness of the importance of hydration. I was thankful to have a strong, healthy body that was able to adequately train and prepare for such an ultimate challenge.

My Ironman experience continued to surprise me. I was asked to do another interview from the same man who initiated my lottery surprise last April. They select some interesting Ironman stories to highlight for local media and they decided to highlight me. The public part of this experience was quite a surprise for me and totally unexpected. Sharing may seem easy to many people, but it is a challenge for my private self. I am more comfortable within myself; this experience helped me learn what it feels like to open up and share.

My Ironman brother, Greg, shared how bad he felt that he could not be in Hawaii for the race and hug me at the finish line. I told him he would be with me during the tough times of the day and I would use his struggle through Ironman Arizona for inspiration during those moments. I may have been doing the physical work, but I realized there was no reason to feel alone when the times would get hard. There were so many people thinking of me and wishing me strength and that knowledge would help carry me through the bumps on my road.

The humility surrounding Kona grew daily. I had changed on the inside when I won the lottery, and it was apparent to a few who were close to me and had shared that my heart had been softened. The Hawaiian culture intensified the spirituality of this endeavor. While in Hawaii years earlier, I was thoroughly drawn to their casual culture, openness and acceptance of others. It was the perfect environment for me, specifically, to take on such a physical, mental and emotional challenge. I felt drawn to the spirit of the competition; not so much to the physical part, as the emotional, soul-searching part. The price I would pay was purely physical, to break myself down to the point of being able to learn about myself in very humble, soulful ways. I tinkered in that humble environment during difficult training days, which made me realize what the actual event could be like.

I experienced so many feelings and emotions while thinking about what lay ahead: excitement, panic, humility, peace, nervousness, innocence, naivety etc. Kona seemed to be always present in my mind. I recognized how nice it would be to hear the starting cannon fire and be thirty minutes into the swim. By that time, my anxiety would be over and I would be comfortably moving forward; finally able to do what I had only been able to think about until then.

I continued to be humbled by what my Ironman experience was doing for me and so many around me. I was pleased with how I had allowed others into my private self and let possible benefits come through my experience to them. I hoped that I could keep my walls down and absorb everything possible throughout my experience. The intensity and single focus of those few months before race day rarely happen in our daily lives. I looked forward to feeling everything associated with my challenge and believed I would receive the same level of rewards as the sacrifices I put into it. My

Ironman was closer to reaching its final chapter and I looked forward to meeting the Andi who would cross the finish line in Hawaii.

> ***Living without Limits:*** *Experiences which seem particularly hard, often nurture camouflaged growth. Sometimes we must humble ourselves to be able to recognize the growth.*

# VISUALIZATION FINDS A HOME

*I prepared to the best of my ability, but until I could be in the actual environment of my challenge, the success of my preparation was really unknown.*

**Saturday**

I flew to Hawaii with my parents and partner. In one week, the cannon would fire and my Hawaii Ironman day would officially begin. A big part of me could hardly wait, while another part was anxious about making the unknown known. It could be an overwhelming thought and, since I was actually in Hawaii, the reality of what I was going to attempt had engulfed my world.

I was nervous to swim in the ocean. It was another unknown for me and I wished I was with a friend who could be in the water with me for moral support. I knew I would be able to do it, but many times it felt like too big of a mental challenge to overcome. I did not like it; there was nothing I was afraid of, I just did not like giving up control while in the water. Overcoming that particular unknown was very important for me.

The most challenging part of my first training day in Hawaii was changing into my swimsuit and heading into the ocean. I don't have a fear of water, but I would really rather not interact with things living within it. I have been able to deal with previous open water swims because I could not see what was in the water with me. Swimming in Hawaii would be different.

My swim was very salty and I could not keep from swallowing some water, which was not pleasant at all. I was puttering along, trying to get used to being able to see my surroundings, when a 10-inch albino fish came into view. It was swimming along the bottom and my instinct was to get out of the water, but I worked through staying in the ocean with the "beautiful" marine-life.

I tried to keep swimming, but quickly decided I did not want to be in that part of the ocean anymore. I got out and walked to a trapped pool of water separated from the actual ocean. I was able to swim more comfortably in that water and felt happy to have my first ocean swim experience out of the way.

**Sunday**

It was a new day and I prepared for my second ocean training swim. I knew it would be better if I swam in the open water, rather than in the trapped pool, but I did not want to deal with being able to see the water get deeper. I decided it was OK to swim in the trapped water because today was simply a training swim.

I made my way, inch by inch into the cool water, until I could put my arms in, then my shoulders, head and finally I could swim. This slow process probably took five minutes, but it is a necessary quirk of mine. Soon enough I was swimming and instantly reminded of the saltiness and the creatures with whom I was sharing the ocean.

There was an island on one end of the area that I stayed away from because I did not want to see its underwater parts. I really wish I could be brave enough to look at non-living things in the water. For example, a big rock suddenly came into view and it startled me. Why in the world would I be startled by a rock? What was the rock going to do to me? It is so frustrating, but a very real thing that happens to me in water.

As my swim progressed, I became accustomed to the terrain I was in. I had seen lots of small fish and only one of the larger fish. When I was on the far side of the island, there were quite a few bigger fish and one in particular took a liking to swimming right under my belly. Yes, it was just like in the ocean documentaries when small fish follow bigger fish or whales, and I did not want this fish to be that close to me. I knew I could not out-swim the fish and, if I slowed down, it would just prolong it being around me, so I kept swimming and the next time I glanced down it was gone. Whew, how stupid would I feel if someone knew I was freaking out on the inside because a fish was stalking me?

During my swim, I discovered that my mind has no boundaries while in the ocean, therefore, it comes up with the weirdest thoughts, followed by a desire to panic and escape at that exact moment. I needed to set some boundaries for this crazy part of my mental-ness. The last thing I needed was a freak-out in the water on Ironman day; that would be sad! Ocean swimming proved to be as big of a challenge as I thought it might be. The next time I swam would be in the actual course, which would make a difference because I would have to deal with what I saw in that water, no matter what it may be.

It was time to fly to the island where the actual race would be held. When I stepped off the airplane, I felt a powerful sense of home and knew I had arrived. I was standing somewhere I had never physically been, yet a part of me recognized the feeling as home and started coming alive. This was the place I had been diligently visualizing during my training and that part of me was hyperaware of what I was there to accomplish.

We drove towards the bike course and my heart was instantly humbled when I saw white rocks spelling out names on the molten black lava. It felt like sacred ground to me. When I rode my bike on it later that day, there was a spiritual feeling surrounding the area that touched my soul. I had to quickly decide if I was going to keep riding and fight back the tears or stop and have a moment. I kept riding and enjoyed the sacred feeling while rolling along.

## Monday

The times I felt in tune with the Ironman spirit were while riding, running, or swimming sections of the actual course. I was ready to focus emotionally on the Ironman and let it take me wherever I went. It had been a long time since I gave up control of my emotions, thoughts, and actions, but I was ready to do so. I asked that the spirit of Ironman be present in me and teach me along my journey. I was ready: spiritually – by humbly respecting the sanctity of this opportunity, mentally – by preparing a plan, and physically – by completing the training. Maybe what I was feeling was the part of me that finally felt it had a home. Arriving in Kona was the key that opened that door.

During a short climb on a training ride, there was a tailwind that must have been the exact speed I was riding because I felt like I was boiling. There was no air movement at all; sweat was pouring down my face, burning my eyes, and my arms were literally dripping. Eventually the wind shifted and the breeze stopped the scalding, but for that moment, I was the hottest I have ever been during a bike ride.

During my training I prepared for an imaginary place, which now was real. The bike course I saw on television really exists, with white rocks spelling names and messages to athletes. The course has a sanctity to it that is palpable. Ironman Hawaii is not just about the physical challenge; it is about digging deep within ourselves and discovering what we are all about. The price is courage, determination and humility. The reward is having limitations removed from our dreams.

## Tuesday

We drove to Kailua Kona to check in and swim the course. I arrived to a very long check-in line which I waited in and saw Chrissie Wellington, the reigning women's Ironman World Champion. She was checking in, just like the rest of us, nothing special for her, other than athletes inviting her to move ahead in line. She is the most gracious, respectable athlete I have met. She hugged the volunteers and let people take photos with her; she was unbelievable. I hoped to be able to thank her in person for who she is, but I knew it would be unlikely.

After checking in, I headed to the swim course to get into the ocean and swim, which is exactly what I did. I slowly walked in the water to get used to the coolness, then put my head in and started swimming. I did not break my stroke until well into my swim. It felt awesome!!! The current really moved me around, but I was able to swim through it. It was a strange sensation to be swimming over a section of coral and suddenly be shifted two feet to the side by the current. Sensing my sudden change of position took some getting used to, but I was able to work through it.

The only thing that startled me during my swim was a scuba diver on the bottom, probably setting up something for race day. That was not something I planned on seeing, but I was able to keep swimming as the startle messages were firing throughout my body.

I heard how important it was to swim the course before race day so you would be used to the beauty and not be distracted. They were not overstating the magnificence of what is in that bay – it was unbelievable. I felt like I was in a beautiful aquarium. My swim was a positive experience; swimming with the Kona fish was much easier than with the Waikiki fish. I fit in with the Kona clan much better.

I walked with the United States athletes during the Parade of Nations which signified the opening of the Ironman World Championship. There were spectators cheering on both sides of the road as we walked by, waving as we passed through. It was an overwhelming feeling to walk along Ali'i Drive and realize that on Saturday, it would be transformed into the world famous Ironman finish line, where I would finish my day. This was the road I had been visualizing for months and I was finally walking along it. It strengthened the genuineness of what I was doing.

**Wednesday**
I helped collect the white coral to be able to spell "Andi" on the lava fields. After really considering where it belonged, I decided on a place just shy of

100 miles into the bike course. I thought I might need something during that section, as things could be quite challenging then. I hoped seeing my name would provide a source of encouragement.

I went to my silly interview, having been one of the athletes they would be following on race day. Thankfully it was short and casual. I asked how they determined who got interviewed and they explained how they sort through a database of hundreds of qualified athletes and then choose a few, based on their personal stories and where they live. I was one of seven athletes from Utah and they decided to target my story for the Utah market.

As I looked through my check-in bag, I noticed my swim cap was purple, which was different than the others. We wondered why and one idea was that they wanted to keep a special eye on the lottery winners, in case something went wrong – like we were not as capable as those who had actually qualified. Leave it to a worrier to come up with that reasoning. Personally, I had no idea why I had a purple swim cap, but during my interview, I learned that my purple cap and fancier, colorful race number were to help the cameramen identify me during the race as an athlete the media was covering. Maybe I would have some unexpected company during the race.

**Thursday**

It was supposed to be my non-training day, but I decided to swim again, just to spend more time in that beautiful bay. I walked slowly into the water and I swam out just as easily as before. It felt great. I had swam quite a distance into the bay when I heard an athlete saying something, so I stopped. It is unusual to hear someone speaking when in the ocean, so I knew something was up. I looked towards the voices to see dolphins right in front of me. I put my face in the water and saw dolphins all around....big ones with their babies, couples swimming side by side, all very graceful and amazing. They were beautiful and watching them underwater was a special experience. One surfaced within three feet of me and I wanted to reach for it, but decided to enjoy the beauty of what was happening naturally.

I continued swimming along the course, hoping to see more. This was an opportunity of a lifetime and I wanted to enjoy it as long as possible. I meandered around and dolphins were everywhere. One was swimming below me, slowly heading towards the surface. I kept swimming the same direction and he continued getting closer to me. He surfaced about two feet in front of me; I reached out and felt the water move as his tail propelled him forward. It was unbelievable. I had no idea this would be part of my Ironman experience.

I finally needed to finish my beautiful training swim in Kailua bay. Dolphins are beautiful, graceful creatures that are said to bring good luck. I am grateful that my hesitancy to be in the ocean did not prevent me from enjoying this amazing experience. What a wonderful reward after conquering something so difficult.

Later that afternoon, I made time to mentally prepare for race day. I found some shade by the ocean and spent time visualizing my Ironman day. It was awesome. Visualizing can be so powerful when preparing for important events. I completed my visualization by signing the Lord's Prayer in Hopi. Tears fell as I imagined, very realistically, what my day would be like and a humble, peaceful feeling engulfed my soul.

**Friday**

I wrote in my diary, "How am I feeling the day before the Ironman World Championship? I feel calm and at peace with what I am about to undertake. Six months of specific training for hot, windy weather will hopefully pay off in the way I have dreamed about. The virtual finish line in front of my home in Utah will be transformed into the Ironman World Championship finish line on Ali'i drive in Kailua-Kona, Hawaii. I am ready to soak it all in and have an experience of my lifetime. I anticipate by overcoming tomorrow's challenges, the Andi who starts swimming may be a different Andi than she who crosses the finish line, many hours later. I already feel my decision to share this experience with my coworkers, friends and family has helped me develop an understanding of how we can affect the lives of others by sharing ourselves. In an email this morning, a good friend shared that I helped him through some difficult therapy this morning as he visualized me swimming in an endless ocean. Sometimes it has been difficult for me to be so open, but I would not change one thing about the last six months, which is a very peaceful, content feeling."

"Kona is finally just beyond tonight's sunset and I am ready for it to be here. My bags and bike are checked in. I have my race day plan in my head, ready to be used. I feel calm and ready for a day of crisis management as my Ironman challenges unfold event-by-event, hour-by-hour, minute-by-minute, and then second-by-second. What an experience that will be! As it has been said before....where else can you have a day you will remember for the rest of your life that does not include a birth, death or wedding? Tomorrow will be that day for me. I guarantee this girl will give it her best, every minute of tomorrow. I have come too far to do anything less!!!!"

***Living without Limits:*** *Give whatever you are involved in the best that you've got. No regrets!*

# IRONMAN WORLD CHAMPIONSHIP

*It was important to remember each step during my day was one step closer to achieving my dream. Regardless of how hard each stroke, pedal or step may have been – each one moved me towards my goal.*

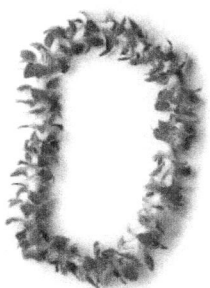

Race day had finally arrived. We walked to where I needed to get body marked and my Ironman spectators needed to claim the perfect place to watch the swim. We gave pre-race hugs and went our separate ways. I got to the body marking area where a volunteer asked for my number. Before I could answer, a gentleman said I was with them. My day with the media had officially begun and it felt strange. They filmed me as number 194 was stamped on both arms and kept filming until I walked through the exit.

The transition area was packed with bikes. I found mine, which happened to be front and center, for everyone standing by the fencing to watch. After I set my bag down, another NBC crew filmed me getting prepared. I pumped up both tires without any problems and put my monitor on my bike, knowing it would record the ride of my life. My bike was ready, so I left the transition area to walk around.

I found a rock wall near the finish area where I could sit and watch spectators and athletes. There was so much excitement in the air and I wished I was with someone, but then decided it was alright to be alone. An older athlete sat next to me who I recognized as one they acknowledged having finished more than ten Ironman Hawaii races. He was eating what appeared to be his breakfast and it made me question if I had eaten enough.

I told myself to stop noticing what he was eating because I didn't want to start out the day questioning my plan. I knew what worked for me and I needed to trust that.

It was time to go back with the athletes and partake of the energetic feeling there. I walked to my bike and stood there for a minute, thinking about what lay ahead and remembering the key parts of my plan. I can only imagine what I must have looked like, because a sweet athlete approached me and asked if I was scared. I learned she was from Colorado, racing for the first time in Hawaii. She was getting nervous and scared and saw me, so came over. Her eyes filled with tears as she shared that she had never done a mass swim start and was really nervous about it. I reminded her to trust her training and that our altitude advantage was going to help us throughout the day. This seemed to help her relax a little bit. I gave her a hug and kissed her on the cheek before she walked away. It was a great athlete-to-athlete moment.

My day became more real as I stood along the edge, listening to the announcer. This part of Kona was extremely different than my previous Ironman experiences because the spectators and athletes were completely separated. It was my first hint of the isolation within this Ironman.

A Hawaiian man sang the National Anthem, which meant my start was getting close. I waited as long as possible, but finally needed to get in the water. I walked down those famous carpeted steps and slowly made my way into the ocean. I looked around at the spectators surrounding us. The starting line was designated by volunteers sitting on surfboards, but I wasn't ready to swim out there yet. I was not in any hurry to get further into the ocean. Finally, the announcer asked that we move towards the start, so I put on my goggles and accepted that it was time to get going.

As I swam towards the start, the announcer was talking, but I wasn't listening to what he was saying. I glanced around and internalized the moment. This was the Hawaii Ironman, the one I watched as a child and thought the participants were crazy. I wondered if children and adults might watch this Ironman and be inspired to change their lives for the better. There is an amazing, inspirational power within this Ironman, which can be quite humbling and illicit gratitude. I am so thankful to have been allowed to share in those feelings.

Without much notice, ready, set, boom……the cannon sounded and we started moving forward.

**The Swim**: The water was as beautiful as it had always been and I was accustomed to most everything within it. I primarily saw fish, scuba divers and a few sinking swim caps. An interesting note is that most of the sinking swim caps were blue, the color the men were wearing, hmm...

For a long time, I felt I was swimming with athletes who were giving each other space. Unfortunately, that feeling went away. At times athletes were on each side of me and, as I approached a slower swimmer, my only escape was to slow down and let them swim ahead, which was fine. I was not trying to set a record in any part of today's race. I remembered my mantra, "just keep swimming".

The last half to the turn-around seemed a bit chaotic. There was a larger guy I could not get away from and it seemed we were always doing the opposite of each other, slowing down/speeding up, veering left/veering right and I wanted to be away from him. I sped up and got away for a while, but soon afterwards he showed up again. I gave up and moved further to my left, hoping to get away from most swimmers. Thankfully it worked.

As I approached the turn-around, the water was the deepest I had seen. It was absolutely crystal blue and the sun's rays were shimmering through it. It was so beautiful and clear. I looked to the side while under water and saw every detail of the athletes near me. Movement seemed to practically stop as I mentally recorded what I was experiencing. It was incredible!

I made it to the first turn buoy and it felt wonderful. There were swimmers around me, but we were not getting in each other's space. The water was still incredibly crystal blue and so beautiful to be in. One particular volunteer, on a yellow surfboard, seemed to be staying close to me and I found it comforting to have him near. I could tell I was getting tired and there was still a long way to swim.

I encountered another volunteer on a surfboard as he zoomed past me. He smiled as he passed and the next time I saw him I slowed up and, within my stroke, splashed water on him. He smiled again. It was a memorable, fun moment to interact with a volunteer while in the ocean.

I started hearing the announcer and wished he was closer. I did not realize I had been veering off course so much, but a volunteer telling me to go left pointed out my unnecessary, zig-zagged swimming. I could go on and on about how long it took to get back to shore, but just know it took a LONG time. I noticed more volunteers along both sides of me and that the route was narrowing, which meant only one thing, I was finally reaching the end of my swim!

I kept swimming until I touched the sandy ocean bottom with my hand, then I stood up and made my way out of the water. The fans were cheering and I was so relieved to get out of the water and head towards my bike, my beloved, comfortable bike.

**Swim to Bike Transition:** I headed to the change tent, found an empty chair and sat down. A volunteer asked if she could help, I said yes. Two more volunteers appeared and started helping me too; they must have needed something to do because most athletes had already been through the transition area and left on their bike – no surprise to me. After all, I was in the water for a long time and this was the World Championship.

I dried my face and my volunteer asked if she could dry my feet. While she dried them, another volunteer put my race belt on and filled my pockets with food. When my feet were nice and dry, she put my socks on, then my shoes. I stood up, felt like I had everything, so I thanked all three volunteers, gave them hugs and went to find my bike. I had no problem finding it, as it seemed to be one of only three or four bikes left. I am not joking; the transition area seemed empty and I could see my bike from far, far away. I got to it and headed towards the bike course start.

**The Bike:** I was on my beloved bike and headed out the chute. I looked to my right and there was my family. It was great to see them because I knew they were as relieved as I was to be out of the ocean. Getting onto my bike was what we all had been waiting for; we knew I would be alright if I made it to that point.

I made my way around the first few miles and rode across a timing mat. It was fun to hear the beep I had become familiar with during Ironman Arizona. I thought of those who would be anxiously awaiting my times at home and was happy to cross the first timing mat for them.

I saw my family again as I approached the busy area. I felt strong and happy, so I popped up and stood to climb the hill ahead. It felt good and, even though it took a bit of extra energy, I wanted to let everyone know I felt great.

As I left my family behind, knowing I would not see them again until I finished, I reminded myself of where I was, riding in the Ironman World Championship with the top triathletes in the world. What an awesome opportunity! I knew this ride held unforeseen challenges and I needed to follow my plan, yet take advantage of being strong on the bike.

I could tell it was humid, but I did well to not let the humidity become a mental challenge for me. I knew I could deal with anything physical as long as I did three things: stayed hydrated, kept ahead on my electrolytes, and paced my nutrition as I had practiced, not too much and not too little.

I made it to the section heading to the turnaround and knew to expect more climbing. Around that time, an NBC sports crew in a red convertible pulled alongside me and asked if they could keep me company. I said I would love a distraction. They filmed me for quite a while; the cameraman would tell the driver to speed up or slow down, depending on the shot he wanted. They filmed from ahead of me, from behind me, from the side and then they were off. It was great to have a distraction for a few minutes.

The wind shifted to a headwind quite some time before the turnaround, so I pushed through the wind, hoping I would get relief with a tailwind after turning around. I finally reached where there were momentary trees and greenery, which was so nice after being in the lava fields for so long. There were actually a few patches of shade to ride through. There had not been any clouds to give us relief from the sun, so the momentary shade felt nice. It was also nice to have spectators on the road again. I saw a woman holding her dog and said hi to the dog. She told me he had come all the way out there just for me. I smiled and thanked her.

I was feeling good and pleased to reach the turnaround, hoping for a tailwind for as long as the Kona gods would allow. This part of the ride was thoroughly enjoyable and I soaked in every second. I looked at the cyclists still fighting the headwind and felt their pain. It had not been an easy ride to that point.

Things were going well until around mile 75. This is when my lesson from the Kona heat and winds started and it did not end for more than 30 miles. The winds shifted from a side wind to a constant headwind that really slowed me down. I tried to focus on keeping my heart rate under control, because I knew this day was not about the bike; I had a marathon ahead. There were still many miles to ride and relief was nowhere to be seen. The sun was beating down and the winds were a steady pressure taking precious energy to fight through. I was riding slowly and then gusts would slow me down even more. I experienced thoughts of being relieved to get off my bike, which was foreign to me because cycling is my strength. It must have been torture for those whose strength was not on the bike.

The aid station at that point only had big water bottles that did not fit on our bikes. I decided not to stop because I felt OK. An athlete in front of me had grabbed one and asked me if I wanted some. I said I was good and he proceeded to dump some on himself. He turned to me again and asked if I was sure I didn't want any. Something inside me told me to take the water, so I said thanks and took it. I drank most of it, but decided it might be good to dump the rest on me.

During my training, I had specifically not poured water on myself because I wanted to be able to ride without doing that. It is not good to get wet when you have to run afterwards. With the humidity, my clothes would not dry and running in wet clothes caused serious chafing. This is why I hesitated to dump water on me, but something told me to dump and thankfully I complied.

I ended up dumping more water on myself than drinking during the remainder of the ride. I am thankful that athlete asked me twice if I wanted water, because I was in my zone and following my plan to perfection. I would have never dumped water on myself unless I was pulled away from my plan and been able to realize how hot it actually was.

I was very careful to avoid thinking about how many miles remained and, instead, focused on landmarks I had visualized. I was digging deep and working hard to maintain my aerodynamic position and speed, but it seemed like I had been doing that for an eternity. The conditions were hard and I knew it because I had been passing athletes earlier, and now was simply trying to maintain my position between two athletes. My next landmark was my white coral "Andi" about nine miles ahead, so I set my mind on reaching that point.

There were quite a few hills to climb and, with the headwind, heat and humidity, it was becoming more of a challenge not to sit up, shift into my easiest gear and just pedal at a granny pace. This part of the ride required I give all that I had and, even that, was only allowing me to maintain a frustratingly slow speed. This was what I imagined Kona might feel like and it had become my reality.

I was ready to be done with the wind and get off my bike. I looked forward and, in the distance, I thought I could see my white "Andi" in the lava field. I focused on that and took in some sort of energy coming from seeing my little, white name in the lava. Tears filled my eyes and I was reminded of what I was attempting to accomplish and that it was expected to be hard. I mentally stepped away from the difficulties of that moment and realized I was following my plan and overall was doing alright. At that moment I felt myself become re-energized. I picked up my pace as I passed my "Andi" and did not have another thought of how difficult it was after that.

I was able to maintain my increased speed and start passing athletes again. I felt for each cyclist I passed; I know it is not fun being passed while struggling. At that point of the day, we all want to get done as soon as possible.

When I was within five miles of the finish, I saw motorcycles surrounding an athlete headed back from their run and I knew it had to be Chrissie, the reigning Women's champion. As I got closer and could tell it was indeed her, I hollered as loud as I could "Go Chrissie!" She didn't break her rhythm, but I was pretty sure she could hear me because of how close I was to her. It was awesome to see her on the course and know she would shortly be the first female to cross the finish line and defend her championship title.

I turned and enjoyed the steep descent. Spectators surrounded the course and I looked to the side and saw my family. It felt good to see them again. I enjoyed being surrounded by spectators and took in the feeling of being back with them; I had missed their energy during the bike.

This particular year was blessed with intense heat, higher-than-normal humidity, and the famous Kona headwinds. The last forty miles felt like I was riding in an inferno with evil, cunning winds, but the bigger challenge was to keep the negative, frustrating thoughts out of my head. Training in the heat and wind accustomed my body to expect a baseline of discomfort, but the Kona gods of wind and fire put my mental strength to the test. This was the most challenging bike ride I have ever experienced and I learned so much by working through every mile of it.

**Bike to Run Transition:** I happily handed my bike to a volunteer and headed to the changing tent where another nice volunteer was ready to help me. Before I knew it there were three wanting to help me and things seemed to be a bit chaotic, so I told them that I was not in a hurry. After sharing that, things settled down and we had a nice transition together. I guess most athletes they helped were probably trying to hurry; after all, this is a race.

They asked if I would like a cold towel to hold to my face. Of course, I said yes. At that point someone also put an ice cold, wet bath towel across my shoulders and it felt wonderful. I changed out of my wet socks, into dry ones, and slipped on my shoes; the dryness felt great. I grabbed my visor, thanked my volunteers and headed out the door. I walked until I crossed the timing mat and then somehow willed my legs to run.

**The Run:** Ironman finishers know the day is really all about the marathon. My plan was to save energy during the bike so I could finish the marathon strongly. I planned to walk every aid station and run between them, no matter how slow my pace might be, because my slow shuffle would ultimately get me to the finish line quicker than walking would.

I saw my family after leaving the transition area and gave them high fives. I could tell how happy they were to see me. I had been out of their sight for over six hours, which I know is hard. I would see them once again before I headed out for the isolated last sixteen miles of the marathon.

There were so many athletes headed towards me who had already run ten miles, so it was hard not to think of how long I had to go. I took a deep breath and had a talk with myself about how it was imperative I only think about the moment I was in. I needed to take this marathon one step at a time.

If I could ever consider running miles tolerable, the first ten miles were just that. There was an overcast of clouds and so many spectators lining the course. I could hardly get the smile off my face. I thanked them for supporting us and in return, they cheered even louder. Many commented on how nice it was to see me still able to smile. It was not hard for me; in fact, the hard thing would have been not smiling, when they were cheering for me during such a challenging event. The spectators made those first miles the most enjoyable they could be. I was happy my energy bank had been topped off, so I could get down to business with the remaining 16.2 miles.

I saw my family as I was approaching the end of those spectator packed miles and gave them a big smile to let them know I was doing alright. Then my running shoes took me out for additional learning experiences in the Kona lava fields. I would not see my family again until I was within the last mile to the finish.

Very soon I would be running on the same road I just finished riding my bike on. The sun was still up and it was nice to run in the daylight. I constantly battled thoughts of walking, so I was thankful my plan included an achievable goal of walking the aid stations and running between them. It helped me focus on my goal, rather than my comfort level, which seemed to work for me.

I started craving cold water and decided to get a glass of ice and try to run with it. I was thankful I was able to do that because it felt so good to have bits of cold water in my mouth. I knew I had to be careful because I did not want to take in too much water. At the first sign of a sloshing stomach, I tossed the ice away, which was hard for my heart to do, but my mind was in control and we did the smart thing.

I was thrilled to pass mile thirteen and be half way done. I remembered the pain I experienced during previous triathlons and took note that the only discomfort I was dealing with was wet shoes and developing blisters. I could not ask for more.

I tried to keep focus on my one mile at a time goal and, before long, I found myself enjoying a beautiful sunset over the ocean. I realized then that every remaining step I could take in daylight was a genuine gift. I wondered what it would feel like to run in the complete darkness. I would find out very soon.

It got darker and darker as I turned towards the energy lab to run down the road which is only open to the public this one day each year. I had heard so much about this section and wished I could see the area I was running through. I had to focus on being careful of where I stepped because the road was uneven and it was so very dark. There were quite a few people walking at this point and I willed my legs to keep up the pace and pass them. I gave myself permission to walk when I was headed out of the energy lab because it would be uphill, but I had to keep running until I got to that point.

There were a few kids along the side of that road, reaching to give me high fives. I held out my hand and slapped each of their small hands as I passed them. As I continued on, I heard them celebrating our exchange. One of them told another to run up and get my number, which made me smile. I find it surprising that more athletes were not interacting with the spectators. I actually gain strength from them and, after hearing what those kids said, I may have left them with a special memory of their Ironman day.

Michael Jackson's Thriller was blaring at the aid station as I ran across a timing mat and made the turn to head back towards Kona. My run out of the energy lab was surprisingly enjoyable. There was a nice breeze and it was cooler with the sun gone. There was a sense of serenity while running in the blackness of the night. I found it peaceful to hear only the slap of my shoes on the pavement, after having been exercising for twelve continuous hours. I had to be careful to not run into any holes or orange cones lining the edge because of how dark it was. In the distance, I could see the red glow of the motivational mile board waiting for me and was excited to see what message my family had submitted.

An interesting part about running out of the energy lab was that I had given myself permission to walk that part, because it was uphill, but I did not think about walking once. Something changed from within me as the darkness engulfed my world. I felt peaceful, serene and stronger as my vision was nullified. I could literally only hear the slap of my shoes on the pavement and I noticed my mind was quiet. The "wanting to walk" thoughts I had been battling were gone.

I was thrilled to pass mile 19 and get closer to the message board. I kept taking steps up the hill, crossed under the Ironman archway where my number was scanned and watched for my message to appear. It took some time to show on the board and, when it finally appeared, I was quite confused. My message read "Good Job Andi, Tadpoles". I had no clue what it meant. I tried to figure out what my loved ones meant by this message, but eventually determined it was not worth the mental energy to do so. I knew they were cheering for me then and that message was meant to be a temporary boost, anyway. Tadpoles? I later found out the message that appeared was totally wrong. The message submitted was "Dreams Become Reality", which would have made much better sense to me than "Tadpoles".

I made it to the aid station at the top of the energy lab road and it was lit up like midday. I got some nutrition and took some ice to munch on. We crossed to the far side of the road and not long after that, the lights of a car approached me slowly from behind. It was a camera crew.

They pulled alongside me and asked if they could light my way. I was pleased to have company and maintained the comfortable pace I had recently discovered. I felt inclined to talk with them and even tried to look at them once, but was blinded by their lights; they eventually asked me to pretend like they were not there. I must have been talking too much. They were with NBC Sports, so maybe there was a chance I would be included in their broadcast, but, on the other hand, perhaps they would not like my smile because it doesn't depict how grueling the day was.

The camera crew left and I was again on my own. It was dark and when occasional headlights headed towards me, I could not see anything. I had to heighten my awareness of my surroundings. I was still feeling a power from within that kept the thoughts of wanting to walk quiet, which gave me a mental break. I needed that break to help me gain strength and prepare for the final miles ahead.

Between aid stations, it was totally dark and quiet. I had only been hearing my own thoughts until, all of a sudden, a man's voice pierced the darkness, with words of encouragement. I could not see anyone and it was pointless to even look in his direction; it was pitch black. He continued encouraging me as I moved by him at my slow, persistent pace. This was something to experience, a penetrating voice from the darkness, telling me that I could do this and that I was a hero to many people whom I would never meet. I actually thanked him out loud. I told him it meant a lot to me that he was there to encourage us at that point of the race. I will always remember those encouraging words, coming from a stranger within the darkness.

Shortly after mile 22, things became difficult again. My familiar thoughts, begging me to walk, reappeared and I noticed annoying pains. I had to dig deep and not give into the difficulties; I was so close to achieving my goal to run between every aid station.

I saw mile 24 and was so happy. I knew I would soon cross to the other side of the road and be that much closer to being done. I could occasionally hear sounds from the finish area and had to smother emerging thoughts of me crossing the finish line; it wasn't time for them yet. I needed all my remaining energy focused on getting through the last two miles.

I made it to the steep part of the course and ran down it knowing the finish area was within my grasp. I ran past the last aid station because I did not need anything except to get to the finish line. The volunteers cheered for me as I pumped my fist in the air. My pace picked up and I am sure my legs were yelling in pain, but I did not feel anything except the pull of that finish line on my soul. The sounds of the finish area got louder with every step and the words became even clearer. I looked to the bottom of the hill and saw my number one fan, Brenda, standing there, anxiously looking towards me. I could feel the width of my smile enlarge as I allowed myself to realize that the moment I had been envisioning for the past six months was just around the corner. As I approached her, she told me I had one mile left and to enjoy every minute of it. I followed the turn of the road and crossed the timing mat signifying my last mile. Only one more!!!

It seemed to take forever to reach the next turn, but I finally got there. I saw an athlete walking ahead of me and I knew I would pass him soon. At this point I was not aware of how fast or how slow I was moving; I was being pulled by a force stronger than my will towards that finish.

I passed the walking athlete and then it was finally me making that final turn onto Ali'i Drive. Two athletes were in front of me and I did not want to be in their moment, so I slowed my pace and took time to high five the spectators standing along the road. They were cheering so loudly and I felt like my face was not wide enough for the smile trying to get out. The song playing was by the Black Eyed Peas, "It's Going to be a Good Night" which was a song I had often envisioned playing at that moment.

I continued towards the finish arch and it was just like I had visualized – the spectators were reaching for me to slap their hands, the music was screaming for me to get across that line and I could feel my dream becoming reality before my eyes. It was better than every virtual finish line in front of my house after those long, hot training days. The spectators made this moment every bit as big as it felt on the inside; the electricity within them was palpable. I ran up the ramp until I was under the archway, then officially crossed the finish line, raised my arms and finally stopped running.

I heard the announcer say loud and clear, "Andi, you are an Ironman!" I raised my arm in the air, acknowledging his words, then looked around to find the person with the orchid leis and made my way down to get my very own Ironman World Championship lei. A volunteer was on each side of me and they laid a towel across my shoulders and asked how I was doing. I told them I felt fine, which was surprisingly the truth. I felt completely wonderful! The moment I crossed that line was unbelievable, overwhelming and such a relief, all at the same time. I did it! I finished the Ironman World Championship in Hawaii!

The volunteers with us immediately after crossing the finish line, are called catchers; an appropriate title for those who literally support us after having given everything to realize our dreams. My catchers guided me through the finish area and made sure I was OK. As we stepped beyond the drapes, I was swept up by my mom who gave me the biggest hug I can remember. It felt good to be wrapped in her arms. My dad was by her side and, after mom loosened her grip around me, I gave him a big hug. My catchers urged me to keep moving, so I complied, with my parents in tow. Not long after we started walking, Brenda found us and there was another big hug. It was great to be back with my family!

My catchers helped me get my finisher medal and could tell I was doing alright, so left me in the capable hands of my loved ones. I thanked both of my catchers and told them to keep up the good work. Now it was just the four of us behind the finish area of the Ironman World Championships in Hawaii. We hardly knew what to do.

Friends and family called to congratulate me and it was wonderful to hear the emotion in their voices and be able to thank them for thinking about me during the day. I felt the strength of so many friends and family and it was good to share that moment with them, whether they were with me in person or in spirit.

I was sitting alone in the recovery area, when a stranger approached me. He shared that I would never know the number of strangers' lives I had touched by accomplishing what I had. For a minute I wondered if he had been on the course and seen me, but he was simply sharing his thoughts because I was there at the right time. He shared that he had finished this Ironman one year ago and knew it was an amazing experience for us as athletes, but even more so for those whom our actions inspired to change their lives. He told me I was a hero to countless number of strangers. It was extraordinary to interact with this fellow Kona finisher and hear his perspective one year after finishing. It was not about the accomplishment of finishing, rather what it does for others. I am so glad he made the effort to share this with me.

I found my family and learned that Chrissie was at the finish. My heart momentarily stopped as I realized what this meant and knew exactly what to do. I dashed towards the finish, hoping she would still be there and that my family could keep up with me.

I found Chrissie, who was talking with some people. I meandered near her and patiently waited for her to finish. At the first hint she was done, I quietly approached her and touched her shoulder. She turned to me, put her hand on my shoulder, looked me square in my eyes and listened to every word I said. I shared my appreciation of who she was and congratulated her on such a challenging accomplishment. She graciously thanked me, kissed me on the cheek and continued with her celebration. I turned to leave, but before I got too far, I closed my eyes and took a moment to internalize what I just experienced. I congratulated Chrissie Wellington face-to-face, in the finish area, as a fellow finisher. What a magnificent, unexpected experience for me.

The energy at the finish was unbelievable. The music was livening; the announcers were masters at engaging the crowd and the spectators were fantastic. Everything felt so alive. They asked the finishers from earlier in the day to stand up, and recognized we were staying to support our fellow athletes still struggling on the course. I am so glad I felt strong enough to be able to stay and cheer for those last finishers. It made a perfect ending to an absolutely miraculous experience.

**Post Kona Thoughts**

People are usually amazed by the Ironman purely on a physical level; the intense mental and emotional challenges often go unnoticed. I do not actually contemplate the physical obstacles because they are predictable and can be planned for. The emotional and mental challenges were unanticipated, in-my-face challenges that took all my determination to overcome. I am honored to have experienced every challenge during my Kona Ironman.

I heard Kona was unique, but I did not expect the amount of intense, soul-centered emotion within it. If I think about the accomplishment entailed within this Ironman, tears instantly fill my eyes. The most powerful emotions surround my memory of returning to my "Andi" in the lava fields, and allowing my intense, raw emotions to tear down the walls still trying to encompass them. I wept as I placed my finisher lei on my "Andi". My thoughtful placement of that white coral on the black lava played a key part during the most difficult point of my ride. Tears had filled my eyes on race day as I struggled past my "Andi" and I felt very strongly I would not be the same person when I returned there. It was an honor to leave my lei as a thank you for what the lava fields did for my soul. They challenged me as I had never been challenged before and changed me forever.

My Kona experience did not end when I left the island; while watching the broadcast of the 2009 Ironman World Championship, I was surprised to see my smiling face come running across the finish line. Yes, my image was immortalized by NBC Sports. It was a perfect closure for my Kona experience.

> ***Living without Limits:*** *When we are truly willing to put forth the effort, our potential to achieve our dreams is infinite. Then, at the pinnacle of the challenge, we may think we are conquering it with our own strength, when actually it is the faith and support of our loved ones' that is keeping us from falling through unseen gaps.*

## ONE LAST NOTE FROM THE AUTHOR

We need to allow ourselves to dream, to try things that may seem impossible. It is haunting that a chemistry class almost prevented me from achieving my dream to become a nurse. By conquering Chemistry, I learned that desire, determination and a willingness to be uncomfortable can obliterate perceived personal limits. I applied that knowledge to my athletic self and was able to finish the pinnacle of one day endurance events, the Ironman World Championship in Hawaii. Don't let your "Chemistry" keep you from achieving whatever your "Ironman" may be.

# ABOUT THE AUTHOR

I do not know why authors write their bio in third person, so allow me try something different. I grew up with four brothers and now live with my partner and best friend, Brenda and Labrador Retrievers, who reluctantly allow me to work as a Surgical ICU nurse. I spend my free time in the mountains, collecting my thoughts on paper, hoping to inspire others to live without limits. I have finished multiple Ironman races, endurance bike rides and marathons, all after turning 40 years old. I live by the motto that age is never an excuse for not chasing our dreams.

Learn more about me at ironmanandi.blogspot.com

# OTHER MOTIVATIONAL BOOKS BY ANDI

**WORLD'S TOUGHEST IRONMAN** – Relying on my newfound confidence from Kona, I finished Ironman St. George in 2011 and 2012 and experienced two completely different challenges, one of which was my mother's worst nightmare. We share each of our perspectives of this day, both of which are very different from the other's.

**LOTTERY WINNER to KONA FINISHER** – A detailed recap and reflection upon my Kona experience, from a perspective of feeling less-than-worthy to participate.

**ONE LAST THING**… if you liked this book, please leave an honest review on Amazon

Made in the USA
Coppell, TX
20 January 2026

69174355R00056